December Roses

December Roses

Pastoral Reflections on Divorce

HECTOR M. MEDINA

RESOURCE *Publications* · Eugene, Oregon

Nihil Obstat
Most Reverend Bishop Kevin Vann JCD, DD
Bishop Diocese of Ft. Worth, Texas

Imprimatur:
Most Reverend Bishop Kevin Vann JCD, DD
Bishop Diocese of Ft. Worth, Texas

REVISED STANDARD VERSION OF THE BIBLE, Old Testament Section, Copy-
right 1952; New Testament Section, First Edition, Copyright 1946; Second Edition
Copyright 1971 by Division of Christian Education of the National Council of the
Churches of Christ in the United States of America.

Resource Publications
An Imprint of Wipf and Stock Publishers
199 W. 8th Ave., Suite 3
Eugene, OR 97401

www.wipfandstock.com

ISBN 13: 978-1-61097-073-0

Manufactured in the U.S.A.

*This book is dedicated to my mom and dad (†)
who grew in their love and commitment
embracing life as one.*

Contents

Foreword

THE TITLE "DECEMBER ROSES" brings to mind the celebration of Our Lady of Guadalupe, the mother of God who appeared to Juan Diego at Tepeyac Hill, and whose appearance brought a time of great faith, conversion, and communion for the Body of Christ in the new world. It was, and is a great gift to all of us. The roses in December which later lead to the revelation of the image of Our Lady of Guadalupe on Juan Diego's *tilma* bring us the image of new life amidst the rocks and barren landscape of snow and winter.

For those of us involved in pastoral ministry, and Tribunal ministry, the challenges couples have faced in marriage and living through trauma, pain, and loss of divorce can be reflected in the barren and rocky landscape of Tepeyac Hill. Our own experience of journeying with people in these moments can be reflected in the real life conversations, experiences, and situations described in these pages. The task and ministry of the reading and studying of marriage cases as Judge, Defender, Advocate, or procurator, in our task of searching for the reality and truth of the nature of consent at the time of marriage, revealed to us real and sometimes violent situations equal to the ones realistically narrated in these pages.

Yet, the power of God in bringing forth new life and communion was shown to us by the presence of the Mother of God and the roses at Tepeyac. So too our experiences of couples being able to enter into a new marriage reflects this new life. So also do the prayers at the end of each chapter. As they call us to see the love and power of Christ present in the lives of couples who seek to embrace the sacramental reality of marriage as created by God.

Let us pray for all of individuals in these pages, all whom we know in their struggles, priests and all involved in family ministry. May those people in these pages and others who "walk through the valley of the shadow of death" also know as St. Paul says that "where sin abounds, grace abounds all the more."

† Bishop Kevin W. Vann, JCD, DD

Acknowledgments

MY MOST SINCERE THANKS to:

Dr. Pat Skarda: Her tremendous editing and personal care of this manuscript has helped to produce an even tighter and stronger voice in behalf of the hurting divorced. Her own spiritual insights motivated me beyond my expectations. She is a blessing God gave to this work.

Ms. Yolanda DuClos: Her corrections and gentle critique helped to provide a sharper image of the couples cited and their addictions. Her diligence and focus helped to shape a cleaner process of thought. Her Christian faith shared in her marriage with Dion is the challenge this work attempts to illustrate when marriage vows are lived healthily.

Sandra Leighton: Her challenge to me in tribunal ministry has proved incalculable. Her personal risks in opening up the pastoral doors of canon law educated me to see people and not cases, the need for healing along with a canonical decision.

My friends at Catholic Divorced Ministry: these men and women have shown me the face of Christ the Healer. They are resurrection and life. NACSDC.ORG

Linda Lawler: My office manager inspires me to continue in many ways as she does the majority of the leg work in producing this material and sharpening my computer skills.

Rev. Carlos Chavez: My best friend's critique, "It makes me want to have a beer and throw myself over a cliff" has been a motivational factor beyond imagination acknowledging that hopefully in this read a tear is shed and new life begins. His insistence that his critique was a good one reminds me why we are friends.

Bishop Kevin Vann JCD, DD: His pastoral concern for the divorced, their hurts and needs, and his personal encouragement in the writing of this book illustrate well a shepherding pastor.

Introduction

THE COUPLE STOOD BEFORE each other seemingly all alone with God. There was no one else in their lives. They knew they were the ministers of the sacrament. Their vows were rooted in their love for each other. Looking into each other's gaze in the flicker of candle flames and the solitude of the moment, they were a blessed sacrament. Their love illumined the small stone chapel. The rings were blessed and exchanged. Gold pieces of metal designed for this moment told the world that these hearts belonged to someone other than themselves, while the inscription inside the ring, pressed daily against the flesh, spoke of a deeper and more profound spiritual commitment to God and to each other. The kiss was the most wonderful expression that marriage had begun for better and for worse.

Only God understood this moment. Only the Lord God understood how this love would challenge all others showcasing the victory and the risks this love dared to challenge. This marriage would be the example and symbol for all to see that love knows no bounds. They were the only couple who ever existed. They were the only couple who knew the intricacies and nuances of the vows. They were the only couple who would last forever against all odds for all time. They were the only couple in the world.

This is a beautiful wedding in all of its appearances. Every detail highlights the fact that two human beings have risked life to enter into a union ripe with possibilities of great joy overcoming great obstacles. It is a spectacular moment which has repeated itself throughout history many times. Couples come before the altar of God holding the person whom they love in their hands, and they profess to all the world that this is the person who makes them whole. At last, screaming to God in exultation like that first being in the tranquil garden of Edenic emotions, one cries out, "this is the bone of my bones, the flesh of my flesh" (Gen 2:23a). This is the person who has put the moon in the sky, the one who shines as bright as the sun. This is the one who stands naked with me and knows no shame. This person is the blessing of life.

Couples enter into these vows ready to encounter and embrace life with all of the optimism of Don Quixote. There will be no complex marital difficulty that they cannot conquer, for they are truly no longer two but one flesh. Any dragon attempting to battle the couple with finances or irresponsibility, adultery or selfishness, machismo or addictions is as unthinkable as roses in December. It is the perfect wedding, but is it the perfect marriage?

Marriage is the scriptural example of the covenant relationship God has with his people (Ezek 16:1–14). The Scriptures are adamant about the fidelity to God mirrored in the marriage relationship (Hosea). The prophets call the people of Israel to return to their spouse the Lord Yahweh while portraying the immensity of God's forgiveness even for the abominable transgression of an adulterous seeking of another love. Husbands are commanded to love their wives as Christ loved the Church (Eph 5:25). Even John, in his exilic apocalyptic vision on Patmos, beholds a new Jerusalem arrayed and adorned like a bride, beautifully ornamented coming to meet her Lord so that even eternity is beheld in the beauty of husband and wife (Rev 21:1–5).

Tragically, however, each day more couples seek a way out of the relationship they desired. Every day, for many different reasons, couples conclude that their marriage was a mistake. The difficulties of committed relationship have soured over time (sometimes days), and the decision of staying in a married relationship is weakened to the point of breaking. No one, certainly not the bride or groom, could have possibly predicted the deteriorating outcome of the marriage.

No one could foresee that the dragons were not some illusory windmills, but that they were actual monsters breathing an all-consuming fire into the lives of these two lovers destroying their achievements and dreams at every juncture. Who would have believed that the fairy-tale prince and princess would lose the castle of their love and not live happily ever after? Who could have known that fidelity and permanence meant two different things to two different people? Who could have foreseen that the kiss in the wedding chapel would loom over their lives until it became a Judas kiss? No one.

Divorce is a reality affecting many people. The couple experiencing the divorce involves everyone around them as they decide publicly to end what they publicly began. As they chose to announce with fanfare and pomp the blending of two lives in the name of love, now because of painful circumstances, they publicly announce with vengeance and rage the disintegration of two lives in the name of anger. This is not the bone of my bones, and any flesh may rot. This is not the person who hangs the moon; this is the person who should be sent to the moon. This is not the sunshine in my life; this is the dark shadow of grief.

When couples marry, they intend it to be for life. Every bride and groom enters into marriage with their own ideas of how it is to be lived. They have rightly or wrongly appropriated their ideas from the families which have reared them. They have witnessed many types of relationships from their parents, relatives, and friends. Each individual has already decided what is right and wrong behavior for a husband or wife based not on his/her own experience so much as on what either has witnessed. Each participant has determined in his/her own mind what he/she will tolerate and what each participant can expect. Each individual has a predetermined mindset about the roles of husband and wife. One of the difficulties is that these mindsets and presumptions exist in the individuals and are not necessarily communicated or shared with the other individual in the relationship. The couple has also set unique mental limits as to what is acceptable in their relationship.

Married couples generally speak of communication as the key ingredient in relationship. It is not always clear or evident, however, whether or not the couple (*i.e.*, both bride and groom) has expressed their ideas of marriage to one another. Even if a couple has been married for years, it is still imperative to examine and re-examine the marriage commitment. Un-communicated expectations about any topic are disastrous. Where marriage is concerned, unstated expectations can kill the relationship at any stage in the process even after years of accommodation and/or tolerance.

Marriage, because it is organic and relational, must be regarded as a process. It is not a one-time stagnant moment in which all time ceases. It is a relationship which, if lived out to its end, grows and develops like a living organism. The relationship can be examined at different stages, and its development can be measured for its healthiness. The process of being married requires a constant examination by both individuals of those simple realities of "for better or worse, richer or poorer, and in sickness and in health." Communication entails more than speaking.

Communication involves the entire person: the physical, the emotional, the sexual, the psychological, and the spiritual.

Tragically, at the beginning, most couples focus their communication on the wedding while the marriage is viewed as a given. With a very limited understanding of communication, couples enter into the process of marriage believing that speaking to one another and coming to agreement on external issues is enough to prepare them for what seems to be a simple thing to do (*i.e.*, to be married). Communication tends to focus on ceremonies, receptions, and apparel while the issues of marriage are left to another time and place.

Since marriage involves the complexity of two human beings, both members of a couple must synthesize their ideas of how they will live out their vows to one another. In the synthesis of lived and loved experience couples forge a marriage in the arena of life. The compromise, the give and take, the doing for the other, allows a couple to rejoice in good times and overcome the difficult ones. It is the knowing of the other person and ministering to his or her needs which allows sickness and health, richness and poverty to be embraced as one until death parts them.

In marriage, each person brings family experience to teach him or her how to behave in a relationship. Couples have seen their parents relate in healthy and unhealthy ways. They have learned their ideas on marriage by what they have witnessed. People grow up in classrooms of love and violence, peace and argumentation, nurturing kindness and abandonment. They have made personal choices from their experiences about how they will imitate and live the roles of husband and wife. Consciously and unconsciously, they will continue in cyclic behavior even if the whole family suffers from it.

When both met their future spouse, they were drawn by certain characteristics and traits of the other individual. The feelings were put into motion, and infatuation was called love. Infatuation planted the seeds for the idea of love. As the relationship becomes more demanding of time and company, marriage becomes an obvious choice: a decision for some, a solution for others. "This is the person I want to be with for the rest of my life. This is the person with whom I want to share myself forever." If there is any opposition from family or friends, it is only because others cannot see the love in the relationship. They do not see him or her as I do. They do not understand the power (and blindness) of love.

Marriage is what comes after the wedding. Marriage is the lived-out experience of "for better or worse, for richer or poorer, and in sickness and in health." Marriage looks to death as being the sole separator of people. Marriage understands itself as being a partnership of two committed individuals working toward the same goals as a couple without losing or dominating another's individuality. Marriage, in cases of mutual nurturing love, looks to the good of the other person. People get married because they are in love with another human being. At the time of their vows, no one else exists for them. People believe wholeheartedly that they will live those vows in total commitment to their spouse, as God is their witness.

As great as this goal is, it is a truer reality that many marriages face tremendous obstacles which some couples cannot conquer. Sometimes the pairing of two individuals does not a good relationship make. The fact that vows are professed before God and community does not necessarily indicate that the vows are understood or that they will be lived. In those moments when the vows are not understood or put into practice, the marriage breaks. Like a pebble thrown into a still lake, a divorce ripples through families touching and shattering everything and everyone in its path.

Divorce leaves no one unscathed. It is not a neutral reality. Friends and families are forced to react. Co-workers and companies are compelled to comment and commiserate. Courts are called upon to divide and deliberate. Children are forced to choose even when they do not want to. Although most couples cannot face the truth about divorce, the reality of it affects many more people than just the husband or wife.

Divorce brings the bitterness of human life to the surface, forcing humanity to ask painful questions about relationships and healing. Like a two-edged sword slicing one couple and challenging the married faithful, divorce desires that all humanity seek fruitful measures of communication in marriage. Every divorce speaks loudly to all remaining married couples. Every divorce is a greater threat to the married as it exposes the real possibility for all marriages if couples refuse to put into daily practice their marriage vows.

Time is no guarantee of a healthy marriage. The length of a marriage is not an indicator of a happy marriage. Length in a marriage does not determine its healthiness. Marriages are made between persons. It is the couple who must decide how they will treat each other. In the treatment of each other, in their mutual understanding of their vows, the couple will forge a married life until death does them part.

When couples refuse to interpret daily those vows with each other, they walk a perilous road tempting and probably hastening the termination of something that they at one time greatly treasured. The consequences of losing sight of the vows with their understanding of permanence and fidelity are overwhelming. To lose sight of the vision of marriage is to risk the pain of selfish arguing, bitter abuse, and at times, hate-filled violence. Losing sight of the vows invites the pain of divorce into a home.

There is an old understanding among the clergy that is passed on to incoming clergy. We tell ourselves, as we stand to take the wedding photograph with the newly married couple, never to stand behind the couple. Photographers usually put the clergy between the bride and groom. Said the older priest to the younger, "Always stand next to the bride or the groom, but never in the middle." "Why not?" asked the younger. The older priest replied, "Because when they divorce, they tear up the wedding picture right down the middle."

Divorce is a sad reality in many families. At times, it is inevitable, as in cases of abuse. Divorce is never, though, a cause of great joy. It is a moment when people are forced to face their lives with very painful truths about beliefs and behaviors. It is a time when their illusions about marriage are challenged to the very core of their beings. Divorce is a moment when the soul, hopelessly lost in self-pity and self-degradation, searches for God in an attempt to heal. These chapters focus on the reality of divorce as lived by different couples. These chapters offer, as well, some pastoral reflections on the relationships of the couples and upon our relationship with God with the hope that they appeal not only to the divorced who seek healing but also to all of us who always stand in need of the mercy of God.

The couples presented in these pages obviously lack certain marital mores noted by the prevalent addictive behaviors, but they challenge us to see a larger picture of life, relationship, marriage, and its termination. Their feelings touch the human in all of us. We are not as removed from these couples as we are close to them. They, in the greatest of their pain, reflect the potential hurt in all of us. Their need for healing is the eternal human quest for the presence of God in human reality (Jer 17:14). The Scriptures remind us God is there knocking on the door (Rev 3:20). Would that we would open the door!

1

I Even Cooked the Supper

IVORCE IS A PLANNED event. It does not happen at random. The one who has chosen to leave the relationship has thought about leaving for some time. For months he will agonize over the how, when, and where, but it is planned. Divorce is a decision sufficiently thought out, debated, argued, and even grieved over in the mind of the one who has had enough of the marriage. For months, sometimes years, a person begins to debate within his own mind the pros and cons of terminating the relationship. Little by little, brick by brick, the house of rationalization and justification is drawn and planned. As the relationship sours, a house of separation is built in the mind of the one who wants to leave. The illusory plans show a beautiful house of freedom, new beginnings, and liberty. This imaginary house is built on the negation of any good in the present relationship.

As in any building construction, the house of freedom is made of sweat and labor, the depressing hurtful grief of reminiscing over the past and losing the present. As a skillful architect draws to the exact inch of a plan, the mind begins to justify what it sees as the only option. The mind asks what has happened to the good times "we used to have." It wants to know when the spouse began to change. "Why isn't he or she the person I used to love?" The mind can even reach the doubt as to whether or not love ever existed.

The mental gymnastics are exhausting. They demand every ounce of emotional strength to be expended in marathons of doubt and confusion. At any given moment, the whistle will blow to jump into the pool of questioning and wonder about the relationship. As fast as it can, the mind will swim into the emotional waters of "why am I staying in this relationship." "Why have I stayed so long?" There is a great fear, as one returns to the dry land of reality, that the whistle will blow again before I have caught my breath. With great anxiety, I shall be submerged into those waters of my past, trying as hard as I can to become better and faster so as not to drown or be slowed down by the waters of "for better or worse, richer or poorer, in sickness and in health."

As tiring as the mental questioning can be, a great prize is awarded at the end of the exercise. Through all the doubting and self-pity, the mind always grants a ten, the coveted gold medal, to the one who is planning on leaving. Being the only contestant, the mind can see no other way out. Enraptured at the gold of self-justification, no one ever sees the trickery that there is no silver or bronze. Mental gymnastics, the exercises of self-arguing over and over in the mind, become an art as one plans on leaving the marriage. The dramatic mental debates, the great argumentative proposals are flawed in that the only one who hears them is the mind of the one who is planning the separation. Simultaneously, the person is the athlete (the only one at that), judge, and scorekeeper. The quixotic mental laurels are given and received while not one spoken word has been communicated to the spouse.

When the relationship worsens, parts of these mental debates will be used as fodder for defense or attack expecting the other party to understand. The expectation can become so great that it will frustrate both parties leading to further anger and rage. Why didn't you, why can't you, and why don't you will become the Trinitarian vocabulary until the marriage ends.

Mental gymnastics, however, are the means by which the person leaving builds enough self confidence to separate. When the art is perfected, the person will confront the marriage as if it never held anything good. Since exercises of mental gymnastics take place regularly, they are structured to negate any good, to focus on the brokenness of the marriage, and to select the day and time when the break will be made. Planning is extremely important in separation. It does not happen spontaneously. Circumstances precede it. Separation, however, does not occur because of one instance of disaffection.

Too many times couples will focus on one issue for the break-up of the marriage without seeing the myriad of situations, which screamed for attention before the separation. At the deepest level of understanding, no one situation breaks up a relationship. Covenants are relationships. People break covenants. People fail to relate. Situations simply expose that failure. The non-communication of expectations and desires heightens the failure.

Couples forget how to play with each other. They stop recreating with each other as they did in their dating period. They stop playing with each other as they did when they were dating. They do not take time out of their married life to be on a date with each other. They do not re-create the relationship somehow feeling that now that they are married, they do not have to do that anymore.

As the instances of non-relationship grow, the desire to leave becomes that much greater. Planning has its roots not in the final instance of divorce or the termination of the marriage. Planning has strong, deep roots. The roots are much deeper reaching back at times even to the wedding. Fertilized with mental gymnastics and instances of non-relationship, those roots provide strength for anyone wanting out of the marriage.

Regardless of any denials, both parties are very aware of the difficulties the relationship is suffering. There is no element of surprise. One party may choose to ignore all of the signs or simply put up with the situation, but upon greater self-reflection, separation is never a surprise. The only surprise is the amazement that separation occurs. The planning to separate creates an emotional time differential for the spouses. Through the constant self-debating and self-rationalization, the planner has fortified his or her emotions giving strength to initiate the break.

The planner has acted out the scene of leaving many times in the mind. She has rehearsed her lines and knows her part very well. She has even anticipated every possible response the spouse might make. In her mind, she has witnessed the tears of her lover, the looks of non-understanding, the endless pleading to try and make it better. She has seen the entire play so many times that she can play every part and quote every line. She has prepared herself well for every possible question that may arise. As in watching the violence or poverty on nightly television news broadcasts, the planner has achieved the total dulling of the senses. She is completely devoid of any feeling of what her spouse feels at the moment. It is a flawed dulling but a negation nonetheless.

The emotional time differential involves the most complex aspects of leaving. It situates both parties at different moments of grieving time and expects them instantly to work out the difference. The one who has planned on leaving has grieved already. She has spent a great amount of time and emotional energy grieving over the loss of the marriage. She is ready to leave and is emotionally at a different stage from her spouse.

She may seem uncaring and callous, but she has spent her emotions beforehand in the gymnasium of her mind. She has already cried all of the tears in her heart. For her, the marriage is dead. As in the case of any corpse, the marriage lies deep within the earthen memories. The marriage is lifeless and merits burial. It has ceased to exist in any positive light for some time now. Like a person infected with cancer, the marriage has slowly died shutting down one organ at a time. It even reeks of death. To stay in the relationship would be comparable to living and sleeping with a dead body. The memories of the relationship, however, may linger.

Like roses in December, the good memories will surface infrequently, but they will tug at the heart and remind the spouse there were times of true love. The majority of memories, however, will slip into rage, anger, and self-justification. Life must go on, even if it costs simple denials of the whole truth.

The other spouse, the receiver of the cruel news that the marriage is over, will be devastated emotionally. It will come as a surprise as he feigns ignorance at any problems so severe in the marriage. The receiver is at the beginning stage of grieving. To the depths of his human soul, he will cry. He will weep at his failure and scream from the pain of human loss to God's deaf ears. There is no balm, no human understanding, nothing which can act as salve for the wound which has been inflicted on him, even though he played a major role as provocateur in it being inflicted. Emotionally, he resembles the devastated Hiroshima after the bomb. At this point, his whole life is over. His world has been annihilated. Every symbol, which guided him, is gone. Every movement that gave meaning to his life has been crippled. He, echoing the great prophet Jeremiah, curses the day he saw light (Jer 20:14–18). From the depths of his heart, his prayer is to be uncreated. Everything that gave him life is gone. The one who shared every act of intimacy has shamed him. Now he stands in the garden alone and not as a couple. Bone of his bones and flesh of his flesh, that which made him whole, has left him naked, and he is shamed (Gen 3:10).

His eyes are now open to the fact that he is a person with feelings, vulnerable, and weak before the rejection of the one who had loved him. Pride may become his loincloth clothing him with masks of indifference in order not to expose the tenderness of the wound within his heart. From the depths of his heart he will scream to God to watch as his eyes stream with tears over the great destruction of his life (Jer 1:16). Only his salty tears will seep into his feelings, and even those tears will burn. Like a wild banshee, he will fly to all of his friends screaming his hurt and seeking anyone who has the power to correct the error that has occurred. No matter how many masks he may wear or how strong he may seem, he is like an open wound exposed to all the elements of life. He is so tender that any touch will cause him to shrink and hurt that much more. His grieving has begun.

This spouse will begin to look for reasons for the break-up of the marriage. He will look for infidelity, a third person to blame. His thoughts will carry him into the inane land of retaliation (for what?). He will begin his own mental gymnastics creating unthinkable situations for reconciliation or revenge. The major difference in these Olympic mental games is that this spouse can never win the gold. It has been removed from his reach. He has run the race and lost. He has fought the good fight and been knocked out. No matter the amount of culpability he holds in the problematic relationship, at this point he is an innocent victim, a child crying, a person needing human touch.

For the first time in his life, he will realize what he has lost. His only desire will be to possess what was his, not understanding yet that people are not possessions. Reconciliation will be the initial mental game. He will concoct every imaginable situation that can occur so as to win the favor of his beloved. He will promise every change possible. He will even accept the blame of the separation. He may actually believe the lie that he is the sole reason for the failure of the marriage. He would like things to be as they used to be without understanding that those things are the events that have spurred the disunion.

Unable to comprehend what is occurring within his own emotional life and totally blind to the fact that his spouse is at a different emotional level after having already grieved, his good intentions at reconciliation quickly turn to rage. Rage and anger provide a much better avenue for his hurt feelings. Rage and anger help to expose the truth that both parties are culpable in this separation. Rage and anger, the forbidden fruits, give the spouse the ability to blame the other person or persons in cases of adultery. At its worst, rage and anger turn to violence.

The open wound hurts so much that it desires its previous lover hurt equally if not more. The rage is so great that it seeks revenge so that the other party can hurt as he does. It wants the one who inflicted this bomb of divorce to be bombed. The feeling of rage wants its lover to be un-loved.

It wants to know that he is crying. After being told that the marriage is over, this spouse (the receiver of the divorce news) has to rebuild from nothing. He did not have the necessary preparation or planning time to prepare himself for the emotional aftermath of his Hiroshima. However, with a full comprehension that he has been devastated, he simply hates.

Hate is a powerful feeling which may consume him until he dies. If hate becomes his feeling of choice, he will live in utter confusion. Hate will be the driving force in his personal physical recovery and the destructive force in his emotional recovery. Hate will lead him to provide for himself in all that he needs, and it will lead him into self-consumption. Hate will be the contributing factor as he argues phantom arguments with phantom ghosts of his lover over the years. Hate will be the means by which he lives and dies.

In the Latino culture there is an attitude that has proven unwavering in its stance. It is the feeling of being *sentido*. There is not a proper English translation, the closest being heartfelt. To be *sentido* is to be so hurt by an action that one becomes immobilized emotionally. To be *sentido* is to be so affected (hurt) in one's heart that the action, which caused that hurt (or the person behind it), is unforgivable. Not even time can erase the memory of the hurt. No apology or absolution has the power to remove the hurt. It is a deliberate stance against forgiveness. The feeling of being *sentido* can even go to the grave where the wounded party will plead his/her case before the Almighty. Being *sentido* is not self-pity. It is an attitude speaking of an unjust action against a human being who seeks justice. The error is that it seeks a justice desiring that another person hurt as "I do." Like hate, it cannot move beyond the self-consuming. A sentido spouse or one filled with consuming hate will nurture and feed feelings of anger and rage with invisible arguments shifting the blame for the separation onto the other.

The emotional time differential that occurs, however, causes both parties to wrestle with dissimilar feelings at the same time. Compounded with many instances of non-communication, it becomes that much more difficult for both parties to communicate and understand the situation before them. Reconciliation may occur at a later date, but only if both parties make personal changes. This is a very difficult thing to realize when at this stage of the time differential both parties have as their goal the desire to change the other person. Each one is so oblivious to the feelings of the other spouse that this blindness becomes the fodder for very heated and hate-filled arguing. Each draws only from the emotions he or she is feeling. Since they are at different stages in the emotional chaos, they speak to one another firing volley after volley of the most penetrating and destructive words which terminate ultimately with the phrase uttered from the pain of the heart: "I hate you."

When lovers fight, they aim for the jugular vein. They fire words of such intense hate that if they were bullets, the other person would be lying in a pool of blood and probably with some of their limbs hacked. They have loved this person in the most intimate of ways. They have shared aspects of life that they have kept secret from all other persons. They know both the intimacy of the bedroom and the public life of being a couple. Sometimes, they have even professed their intimacy before God inviting the Divine to share in the union of their souls as if their love has surpassed the Divine Love. They have loved in every way possible. Therefore, when an argument occurs, the ammunition available to bombard the other person is abundant. Past hurts and resentments are fired at each other shelling the other party but from different emotional barricades. One volley comes from the planner while the other volley is fired in response from the current mourner. Hate-filled emotional memories fill hundreds of households with the attackers never realizing that they are at different emotional vantage points. In this battle, the planner is always the winner because no matter how much hate is fired, no matter how much his emotions have been besieged, no matter how bloody his memories, he has grieved and can leave. "Hate me; hit me; hurt me; I am leaving this marriage." Planning always has its rewards.

CASE STUDY

The couple had been married for fourteen years but had known each other for close to eighteen years. Their intimate relationship had begun years prior to the wedding. The husband had decided he wanted out of the marriage. Many of the tell-tale situations had been in front of both of them for years. In the early years of marriage, they had learned to communicate with each other in overcoming many obstacles, but somewhere in the relationship, they stopped talking to each other honestly. Both fell into the trap of expecting the other to read their hidden thoughts and busy minds. One day he came home from work. The husband was tired, but today was the day he had chosen to leave. Coming in from his own long day at work, his spouse had no inkling leaving was on his mind. They greeted each other with a kiss which hindsight would later label the Judas kiss.

Seeing his exhaustion, the spouse decided that they would stay in to dine and she would cook his favorite vegetarian meal. A steaming pot of white rice and a hot wok filled with vegetables sautéed in butter and white wine and covered in aromatic Chinese spices gave the kitchen a wonderful smell. The dutiful spouse filled a plate with the rice and doused unsparingly the tender veggies on top. The plate was brought to the husband sitting on the floor in the living room watching television.

They said grace. "Gracious God," began the husband with a prayer hypocritically lauding the Lord with thanks for the food and for his spouse. He ate everything on the plate and was not shy about seconds. His face beamed with satisfaction. The meal was "excellent," he said. "It's just what I needed. It was delicious." The next morning leaving for work, he gave his spouse a kiss, and said, "Take care of yourself," knowing full well he was never to return to the house again. Days after as divorce became the reality, the abandoned spouse in a furious rage realized the divine irony of the situation. "I even cooked him supper," the spouse said with a true belief in the fantasy that a simple meal made out of love to satisfy the husband should serve as a deterrent to any desire of leaving. It was an elegant last supper, and echoing the stories of the Gospel, a profound ignorance of the crucifixion lurking in the shadows.

PASTORAL REFLECTION

Honesty is the key ingredient in any relationship. Honesty acknowledges the dignity of humanity. Jesus, who is the Way, the Truth, and the Life (John. 14:6), lived in honesty with those whom he encountered no matter how harsh the truth. It was his truth, which confounded the disciples as to whom held the guilt in the blindness of a man (John 9). They so wanted to blame him or his parents while Jesus desired that God be praised and glorified in all things even sickness. It was the truth within Jesus that allowed him to have his feet washed with tears of a sinful woman while Simon and the Pharisees held mental courts of self-righteousness (Luke 7:36–50). It was the truth of the Lord, which could call fishermen and court women to come and follow him as disciples. It was the truth within Jesus, which gave him the freedom to lambaste the Pharisees and Sadducees for their hypocrisy. Even in his condemnations of their lack of faith and practice, he truthfully desired their conversion (Luke 15). Ultimately, it is Jesus in complete honesty with himself who can look down from a cross at people filled with hate and ask his father to forgive. Honesty makes one free.

The truth, though, can be a scary reality. Truth will demand a self-examination walk, which few attempt. Truth comes in many different shades and colors, but ultimately, it is the truth of self that frightens us most. Honesty acknowledges the beauty of the creative force of truth. Honesty in relationships acknowledges the beauty of the other human being. Jesus' words against pharisaical hypocrisy have their base in his desire that the Pharisees would recover the beauty of their faith: to seek and live according to the righteousness of God instead of their self-righteousness. Honesty continually battles against the forces of tact, diplomacy, pretentiousness and deceptive practices even when these forms are purported to be done for the good. Scriptures call for a "yes" to be a "yes" and a "no" a "no." Scriptures make the claim that anything else has evil as its root (Matt 5:37). We are afraid that if the truth were spoken someone (maybe even myself) may be hurt.

The husband knew very well his decision to walk out of the marriage. He had planned the moment long ago. His lack of honesty, even with himself, did not allow him to speak to his spouse of the truth of his feelings. His prayer before the meal, routinized and dishonest in his blessing for his spouse, illustrates the depth of fear when one forsakes honesty for tact. It is not so much that his dishonesty affects the spouse. It does. But at a deeper psychological level, the husband has deceived himself into believing that he can just leave.

It would have been to the healing advantage of both if he had been honest with his feelings and faced a confrontation that night. It would have been better if he had believed his own prayer: that God is gracious and that both he and his spouse live in God's grace. It would have been honest to acknowledge the humanity of his spouse no matter how painful a situation might have been created from telling the truth. In all of his planning to leave the marriage, truth was relegated to a darkened corner for the husband. The hurt generated by his action is incomprehensible. Truth had been the strength in the marriage. When did the couple decide that it was more prudent to live contrary to the truth? When truth was needed the most, the husband chose a lie.

The spouse too cannot feign ignorance. It was no secret that there were problems in the marriage. The fact that the couple attempted very little to correct them was evident as well. Communication had once been their most valuable asset. Each one decided to deceive him or herself without realizing the devastating effects that would occur. The irony is not that the spouse cooked the husband his favorite vegetarian meal. The irony lies in the fact that each one had the capability to discern the signs of the times and failed to evaluate the marriage honestly.

Jesus is the best example of honesty. In the garden of his agony, he even tells his father his fears about dying. He is not afraid to question or ask. He is not afraid to hear the voice of his father challenging him to risk everything for the truth of divine love. All relationships thrive when honesty is at the core. In ministering to his people, Jesus told them the truth about life and left it in their hands to decide for themselves what they would do with that truth. So attuned to the voice of his father, Jesus would choose death rather than forsake the truth for a lie.

By his life, passion, death, and resurrection Jesus has prepared an immense banquet for us in the house of the Father. He continues to feed us with his Body and Blood giving us a foretaste of the eternal union to come. I wonder how many times we have planned our escape from the relationship he desires with us. We have committed ourselves to him over the years in so many ways. Each one of us knows, however, the times we have prayed our prayers of graciousness, knowing very well our plans of walking in other paths. In simple reflection, I can hear the voice of the Lord pleading for a faithful covenant with us. The meal has been prepared. The prayer has been raised. All that is left is the truthfulness of our covenant with him.

PRAYER FOR TRUTHFULNESS

Lord God, author of all truth,
You alone, Lord, see the depth of my hurt.
You alone have heard my tears in the night.
You know my deceit
to myself and to others.
You know my weaknesses.

Lord God, author of all truth,
You know the lies of my life,
the ones I have told,
the ones told to me.
You alone have the power
to remove the web of deceit
to breathe in me the spirit of truth.

Lord God, author of all truth,
teach me not to lie
to myself
or to others.
Be gentle to me
that I may grow in your grace
and dwell in your truth,
that I may heal.

2

When I Have Cancer

IVORCE HURTS. THE SEPARATION or breaking of the relationship is
extremely painful. One appropriate image of divorce is a beautiful
crystal bowl being smashed onto the floor into tiny pieces, forever irreparable. Couples may reconcile, but it is never the same crystal bowl. It
cannot be. The smashed bowl leaves everyone wondering where to walk
without getting sliced by slivers of what once was whole. People are forced
to comment on the brokenness. Perhaps it was never a pretty bowl in the
beginning. Perhaps one spouse or the other or even a family member
knew it wouldn't last. Perhaps everyone wonders who will clean up this
mess. "I told you how he was." This bowl was in our family for years, and
now it is irrevocably broken. Sweep this up, and place it in the trash so
that no one else will get hurt. What happened to that bowl? What happened to the marriage? Who broke it?

Marriages, however, are not as carefully designed and well-fashioned
as crystal bowls. Fine crystal has its impurities burned out in scorching
fiery ovens. Fine crystal is treated and purified because its maker desires
his every creation to be a showcase of pure perfection. Fine crystal has no
feelings.

Marriages involve a rich complexity of human feelings. Marriages
demand what inanimate objects cannot. Marriages demand human attention and touch. They seek out human involvement and commitment.
They necessitate a response to being. Marriages fail for many reasons, but
at the core of the failure is the failure to communicate expectations. After
a certain amount of time, married couples expect their spouses to intuit
just about everything. When one party decides that the other should be
able to read his/her mind and anticipate needs that is the moment when
problems will arise.

For some couples, fracturing begins as soon as the marriage does. For other couples, differences become insurmountable over the years. Sometimes couples, as they spend more time together, speak as if longevity has somehow miraculously provided them with the gift of knowing what a spouse wants. "I know exactly what he is going to say." "I know exactly what she wants." At times, this is even spoken of as a good when in reality, thinking and acting in this manner tends to reduce the individuality of the spouse. As the individuality diminishes, people are usually taken for granted.

When one spouse fails in reading the other spouse's mind, desired results never occur; then deep resentment and frustration become part of the marriage. Spouses, at times, are expected to be able to read the other's mind or to anticipate the silent and often capricious whims of the other party. The ability to intuit and anticipate correctly does not occur as often as most people would like to believe. It is an exasperating exercise in inanity. It is easier to read Tarot cards than to read the mind of a spouse. The Tarot, at least, is colorful and imaginative and has set rules of interpretation.

As spouses grow in expectation that the other one will anticipate his/her needs and wants, both parties create the atmosphere for very explosive and hateful situations. When expectations are not communicated, not only is there the potential for confrontation, but there is also the underlying desire of control. Expectations, which are not communicated, rest in the domain of control. Unstated expectations give one party the power to try and control the other by capricious whims so that no one is actually satisfied.

When there is no communication of desires between spouses, and one party still insists that the other should serve his or her hidden expectations, then that party is in a control mode. He sets the stage of fantasizing in his own mind: If my spouse loves me, then my spouse should know what I want without my telling her. This spouse is setting the stage for his own fall. Control is the hidden issue. The unsuspecting spouse, clairvoyant as a piece of granite, has no chance of winning. One spouse is always at the mercy of the mind of the other spouse. When he fails to intuit, he is damned. When he intuits correctly, it will be insufficient. It is not uncommon for spouses to use a philosophy of "you should be able to read my mind" in their relationships. Then to heighten matters and make them worse, couples will attach the quality of love to the un-communicated expectation. "If he loves me, then he should have known what I wanted."

All couples engage in this form of non-communication. Even healthy marriages play this dangerous game.

When it is played, love becomes diminished. Love seeks the good of the other person. This game attempts to control the other person. Control does not allow for the expression of feelings. It does not respect the individuality or humanity of the other person. Trying to control another human being does not allow for the much larger vision of human relationship. Couples love each other because at one time they were attracted to the individuality of the other person. As their relationship sours, they attempt to murder the very individuality they loved in the beginning. The vow that the two shall become one flesh does not imply that one party shall dominate the feelings or behavior of the other party. It does not mean that one spouse shall control the thoughts and emotions of the other.

Control focuses on issues. Issues isolate couples and do not allow them to breathe the air of a broader relationship. Issues suffocate couples as they force either husband or wife to limit creativity and fantasy. Issues are the offspring of control. Similar to its mother control, issues desire a win with the prize being to control the behavior of another human being. As numerous as issues are, there is never one issue which is the sole reason for the break up of the marriage, though issues can localize the un-restricted un-communicated expectation.

Issues in a marriage are hardly the cause of the disunion. They are the symptoms of the diseased union. They are the arrows pointing to the fragility of the relationship. Issues expose the strengths and weaknesses of any relationship. Issues are clear windows that allow us to see how people speak and interact with each other. They are the evidence that masks deeper -rooted desires and problems in the relationship. Issues (*e.g.*, immaturity, sexual addictions, child abuse) are the headlights illuminating the frightened deer in the middle of the interpersonal communication road. Issues (*e.g.*, finances, in-laws, job loss) disguise the underlying feelings that refuse to surface or be communicated. Issues (*e.g.*, adultery, alcoholism, addictions) help the couple to walk in huge circles without ever confronting the real reasons or feelings buried deep within them. Focusing on issues, rather than the strong undercurrents of feelings, gives the couple permission to carry on for years hurting each other without facing what needs to be addressed. Issues go hand in hand with the desire to control another human being. Without ever facing the problem of control and acceptance, issues allow the couple to move from one issue to another. Moving from issue to issue allows the blaming to continue as each side racks up points as to how many issues each one can enumerate and win.

There is a joke in Spanish that speaks of a farmer whose wife was an incessant adulteress, a true nymphomaniac. She would have sex with every man available. The farmer would move from town to town. In each town, the wife would meet any man available and have sex with him. When the farmer finally had enough of her adultery, he would move to another town. There she would engage all over again in her infidelity. On one occasion, as they were changing to another town, the farmer was pulling his cow. The cow, however, began to moo. "Mooooo," said the cow, and it would not move. "Mooooo," it said again and would not budge. The moos continued with such a sorrow that finally the wife who was walking ahead of her husband and cow, stopped in her tracks. She could hear the moos very clearly. Slowly she turned around and stepped in front of the cow. Bending over, she looked the cow in the face and said, "Don't be so sad dear cow. There is no reason for all your mooing. There will be plenty of bulls in the next town."

Couples whose marriages are in danger love to travel from issue to issue. Focusing on different issues allows the couple to avoid having to face the deeper feelings behind the issues. As in the case of the farmer, it is easier to deny the problem than to face the reality. It is difficult to tie couples down to the deeper-rooted feelings. Traveling around the issue spectrum allows the couple time to fire their volleys and re-load their armaments with even stronger and more deadly ammunition. Tasting every issue, as a child in a candy store, gives couples permission to avoid the reality that issues are made out of a response to feelings.

Moving from issue to issue is a game of one-upmanship as couples rack up their points and counter points to invisible judges of reason and fair play. The entire game of issue enumerating is based on the desire to win, to be right at all costs. Issue enumeration denies the humanity of the other person. It seeks only the triumph of its own position. It has, as its goal, control over the entire game board.

Issue enumeration is comparable to a prolonged chess game. Foolish issues (extended family or who paid what bill) serve as pawns advancing toward the other side of the chess board while protecting the greater issues, the more powerful and more deadly. At any given point in the argument, one can hear the call "check" and watch as the other party shrinks and is usually futile in the attempt to block.

As couples set argumentative traps for each other, it is not surprising when a powerful deadly issue whisks across the board to annihilate the unsuspecting opponent. The powerful queen issue (the unwanted pregnancy before marriage) that has initiated the problems of the marriage since its inception, is always ready to destroy. Lurking patiently, she awaits the proper move to pounce upon her victim mutilating any defense.

The agile knight issues (immaturity, finances, or irresponsibility) with his ever-beautiful and dashing horsemanship allowing the player to jump over the trivialities of the marriage difficulties, are always present for the graceful equine surprise attack. Lest any spouse forget his sins of infidelity or abuse in the years of the relationship or how holy vows before God have been violated, there is always the bishop issue ready with his crosier of religious righteousness to use more as a kung-fu bamboo staff than any type of pastoral implement. As each spouse castles to strengthen a position, any hope for understanding or hearing becomes lost in the quest for supremacy. Issue enumeration is endless.

The inherent error, though, in issue enumeration is no single issue or number of issues is sufficient to elicit the necessary checkmate. The prolonged chess game is never ending because as each party refuses to listen to the other, checkmate is unattainable. Since issues are the masks couples wear to hide their innermost feelings, the chess pieces of issues simply continue to battle each other, striking blow after blow in an un-ending game bent on hurting the other individual in order to be right. In the background sits a silent king issue questioning the very existence of love. It is, however, of no importance that no checkmate is ever declared. It was never a chess game in the beginning. It was the human life and interaction of two people.

Issues illustrate the complexity of non-interaction. They display the reality that people do not communicate their feelings. Issues focus on the rage that comes with any injustice. Issues revel in anger and draw their strength from the fury of the topic. Couples focusing on issues, instead of feelings, are appealing to the gods of logic and reason to enter into the realm of the debate in order to prove a point. Couples, because of the intensity of the anger, never realize that nothing is gained by winning the argument on any issue. Did any mutual behavior change? Did any mutual constructive communication occur? Were any feelings besides anger manifested?

Mutuality is the key. Focusing on issues does not have as its goal mutual change. Issues desire that one party change his or her behavior while ignoring the mutual interaction of two people. The vows of marriage involve two people. For better or worse, richer or poorer, implies two people working toward the same goals. Mutuality in a marriage does not mean that life should be better for one spouse and worse for the other. Mutuality negates any flawed conception that one spouse should live richly while the other suffers from poverty. Mutuality seeks the good of the other person. Mutuality has no understanding of the "me" language.

One night, I sat at supper with two couples, one heterosexual and the other a gay couple who had been together for about thirteen years. At the supper table, the daughter of the heterosexual couple started distributing pictures of her graduation from high school. She gave one to her gay uncle who placed it silently on the table without realizing it was a gift. As the dinner conversation progressed, the gay uncle picked up the picture and gave it to his mate. "This is ours," he told his spouse. "This is for our house." The girl's father and the gay uncle were brothers. Her mother looked at me with appealing eyes. Her eyes were demanding answers, but it was not the appropriate time to ask the questions.

Later in privacy, we talked, and she stated that she wanted what the gay couple had. She said, "Did you hear him [the gay uncle]? He said 'our' picture, 'our' house." Her musings were that her own husband of twenty-two years still had difficulty referring to things as "ours." He more often than not spoke in the "me" language until later it became a joke to speak of "me-mi-mo-mu." The gay couple had learned a secret, a very important one, to a healthy relationship. The oddity is that gay couples have no social structure to encourage the "our" language. Society still refuses to legitimize their relationships. Their attempts at mutuality are drawn from the desire to establish their love with each other every day. For years without societal approbation or sanction, many gay couples have shamed the heterosexual world by living faithfully what others profess publicly, legally. This particular gay couple may have its own difficulties, but it was very evident that they had mastered an important tool of mutuality. Healthy relationships are based in the "our" language.

Mutuality speaks of "our" marriage, "our" relationship. "Our" is a hallmark of healthy marriages which seek to communicate feelings, needs, and wants. Mutuality has as its vision the reality that by loving my spouse, I love my very self. Cleaning "our" house, paying "our" bills, raising "our" children, living off of "our" incomes, or rejoicing over "our" picture exercise mutuality. Mutuality neutralizes any notion of separateness while not losing the beauty of individuality. Mutuality acknowledges that any issue involves behavior of two parties. Although it may be easier to focus on the sins of one party, an even greater error lies in the refusal to recognize that two people are involved. Whatever issue may arise in the deteriorating relationship, it involves both parties even though that may not be apparent at the beginning. Adultery is the result of the interaction of three people not just two. Issues tend to ignore the mutuality of the marriage vows. Issues do not have as their concern anything but the isolated subject matter. Issues, in a masturbatory manner, focus entirely on the topic at hand. The pleasure is in the win, and it is solely a self-pleasure. It is selfish.

CASE STUDY

The couple began its relationship on a totally sexual level. Infatuation and all of the sexual antics provided the background and foreground of their relationship. Two very strong-willed personalities were both opinionated by nature and experts in argumentative debate. Their backgrounds clashed many times in the early years, but the sexual lovemaking was so satisfying that they began to pledge their love to each other. Each one romanced the other many times with very explicit sexual gifts, cards, and letters. It was a relationship based on sex. In their situation confusing sex and love was not uncommon, but because of their mutual intelligence, they could usually act beyond their difficulties. Fidelity was never a strong component in the early years. It would prove to be even weaker in the latter years of the marriage. Their mutual pardons and mutual secrets gave very confusing messages to both of them. At times, they were more in lust with each other than in love.

Fantasies and sexual play bound them together. They were no strangers to sex, at times even inviting (or seducing) a third party for their own antics. Three-way sex occurred before and during the marriage. At one point in the marriage, they graduated to a foursome. When they were engaged in the orgy of sex with their multiple partners, they did it together. It was as if they were going to a movie together. These extra sexual moments never caused them any doubts about their love for each other. They loved sex. The couple married, and the strong sexual connection continued.

Usually they could see beyond their issues and face the feelings. They could detect the causes of their arguments and work through to reconciliation. At one point, they did love each other. It was not, however, at the beginning of the relationship. In an unusual way, they had taught themselves how to satisfy the other person. Their constant sexual play had taught them how to please the other person. They defined this as love.

At the time of the break up of the marriage, they were facing many issues, and they had forgotten how to communicate their feelings. They had begun to play the issue enumeration game. They had forgotten the power of dealing honestly with their feelings until they began to confuse the issues with their feelings. Although both had professed a never-ending love, it was easy to see they had major problems and neither one wanted to face them.

Because of their ability to speak honestly about feelings and desires, to this day they have the capability to reconcile or at least move to a point of peace within their lives, but it will not happen in the near future if at all. At the time of the disunion, even their sexual playing had become routine. Lusting never ends, but the lusting for each other had ended for many different reasons. Like the seed sown on rocky ground, their relationship had few roots (Matt 13:5). When the sun rose at its midpoint, it scorched the couple, and they realized the shallowness of their intimacy.

As the years of marriage continued, they started to move toward distinctly different philosophies of relationship and marriage. They forgot to speak of their feelings and desires. Their sexual play was practically non-existent. When they did have sex, it became routine, a duty not a pleasure.

One spouse began to gain weight and to diet vigorously in a never-ending cycle of gaining and losing. The husband was very critical of overweight people, making horrible passive aggressive remarks about fat issues. It was an obsession with him. He would remark how unhealthy a fat person is or make an illogical leap to say that incompetence in the workplace usually occurred because the employee was fat. Any mistake or error in any subject was due as a result of being fat. People had hemorrhoids because their butt cheeks were too fat. Typos in documents were the result of fat fingers. People had low self-esteem because of their fat.

As the spouse listened to the endless tirades on fat and fat people, it was not that difficult to understand to whom her husband was indirectly referring. The spouse went on diets and would lose weight only to regain it. She would be frustrated losing weight without any response from the husband. The husband at times would not even notice. When the spouse was fat, however, the husband would make it understood indirectly that it was not to his liking. Periodically he would try to broach the subject with the spouse. Feigning concern for the health of his spouse, he would talk about getting fat. Because of all of the other passive aggressive statements that had preceded the truth session, the fat spouse usually could not hear any genuine concern or truth in any statement on fat.

After not seeing the in-laws for some time, the couple went for a quick visit. The alcoholic father-in-law looked at the spouse and in his usual uncaring manner bluntly asked, "When did you get so fat?" The couple stared at each other. God does take care of fools and drunks. All in all, weight was dealt with as an issue, though, with neither of them examining their feelings. Even in the sexual act, after needs had been satisfied, the husband would grab his spouse's stomach never saying one word. He didn't have to; the fat said it all.

In their younger years, they were a very handsome couple. Dancing together, they were superb. They would dance the country western dances with the best of dancers. They were sassy in attitude and used each other's intelligence to point out the ignorance of other people. At times, they would dress provocatively knowing that it brought a sensual pleasure to the other spouse and on a dance floor, they demanded that all couples notice them. Dressing in the same patterns and colors heightened the fact of their being together even in situations that called them to pretend not to be together. It did not matter to them. Their own sensuality and sexual coquettishness allowed them to challenge and conquer the morés of society. Their dancing proved to be wonderful moments of memory for the both of them. With added alcohol, they seemed to dance as one. Entwined with themselves and infatuated with the youth of life, on a crowded dance floor, they were the only couple. Watching them from the neutrality of the benches, it was obvious that this couple coupled. Dancing was to be a significant key that the weight issue was not being addressed in honesty.

One night, when the couple went dancing, the husband found it difficult to move his beloved to the music. There was much more to grab, but it was difficult to move. Both of them knew what was occurring but said nothing. The couple could not keep the beat. The husband refused to dance anymore excusing himself with lies of not feeling like dancing. Why? The alcohol could not even give an appropriate answer.

At a later date, hidden in an island karaoke bar, the spouse demanded a dance from the husband who remarked to his sister and brother-in-law that "the last time we tried this it didn't go so well." The couple did fine as far as the dancing was concerned, but it was evident the husband had his heart in other matters. The overweight spouse was proud the dancing went smoothly thinking the three pounds of water weight shed the week before were the answer.

On vacation, the weight issue would become intolerable. One morning, the last day of the trip, the husband cuddled up to his spouse and related how he had tried to have sex with another individual in the bed and breakfast the night before. As his spouse was sleeping the husband went, flirted, and propositioned someone else. He was turned down because the other individual knew he was a married man. Trying to be as honest as he could, he offered a rationale as to why his spouse the night before had refused to participate in a sexual game at one of the local clubs.

"I think you didn't want to play the game because you were embarrassed by your weight. I have not attended to your sexual needs because of the extra weight. It bothers me. I know I do not have oral sex with you for that reason. I think that's why I went looking for sex with someone else." For the first time in many years, the husband was honest. A silent spouse could hear the heart breaking as physical and emotional rejection combined into reality. Then the husband, in the shallowness of his warped ego, cuddled closely to his spouse and petitioned sex.

Unable to see the tear rolling from the spouse's eye, and without a clue that he had inherited his father's insensitivity, he tried to have sex with his spouse. In his complete self-absorption, he was his father's son. The spouse said no. "I am not at the mercy of your charity. I am not a whore."

Ashamed to the core of the soul, the spouse could not bear to be with the husband in any fashion, but being on vacation, there was no way out. Grin and bear it. Nurse your soul. One more day to go.

"I remember so clearly that moment of not being loved for me. I realized right then and there that no one loved me. Do you know how lonely that is? I even asked myself if I loved me. I remember wanting to write myself a card and mail it to me so that upon my return I would find a note from myself encouraging me to love myself. I know this sounds stupid, but I think it was God trying his best to remind me that he loved me. I could hear my tears inside my head, and I could not silence the pain of human loss. I saw myself in my mind shrinking into a fetal position.

I was in the garden, naked, and ashamed, so I hid myself so that I would not have to see how much I hurt (Gen 3:10). I had so many things to face. I had to see the individual my husband desired at the breakfast table that morning and pretend some foolish game I had won when in reality I was not even a contestant. I had to continue the vacation walking the scenic plazas when my soul wanted to hide (from me) and cry. I had to eat lunch. In my life I have experienced moments of great pain, but never have I felt as cheap and worthless as that morning. I loved him. I am so stupid. After all of those years, after everything we had done, I thought he loved ME."

That night in a different club but with the same alcohol, the spouse told the husband in Spanish of a long past infidelity. The Anglo husband was furious and angry. The spouse only wanted to clear the air about the adultery, saying it had nothing to do with the incident in the morning. As they talked and drank, the spouse told of other infidelities. The weight issue jumped to the adultery issue, and from that very moment, divorce became an even greater option for the husband. Adultery became tit for tat as the husband began to cheat on his spouse, perhaps in retaliation or perhaps because of weight. Sleeping with other people was now on an individual basis and not as couple. Some seed fell on rocky soil.

The couple divorced amicably, if there is such a thing. They even spoke of searching for reasons for the spouse's adultery. It would probably have proven more profitable if they had broached the subject of infidelity, which is a much wider avenue than a sexual act of adultery. The husband had often gone home with other people because of his drinking but was emphatic that nothing sexual had occurred. Filled with alcohol, how would he know? He did know, however, that his spouse disapproved of his sleeping around with other people. For all of their sexual liberty, even the spouse realized that the husband's personal drinking behavior was a denial and exclusion of her. Perhaps both parties could have realized their share in the infidelity.

Amicable divorce does not remove the pain or the grief of what was. Divorce hurts. It penetrates the soul of a human being and watches it bleed. The spouse remarked openly in an intense moment of grief, "I hope that one day I will suffer from cancer. When I have cancer, my ex-husband will come to see me and wish me well. He will come with flowers and pity. I will look him in the face when he walks into my room and from my bedside my body too weak to even lift my head, I will tell him:

"Am I skinny enough for you now?' Then I will call security and have him thrown out of my room."

PASTORAL REFLECTION

When we make impossible demands on our lives, we continue to bind ourselves to the chains of sin and death. Jesus, in the beauty of his resurrection, broke those bonds of sin and death that we might have life: life in abundance (John 10:10). We, who are graced by the resurrection, find ourselves at the crossroads of doubt so often because of our refusal to hear the Gospel speaking about our life. The Gospel is meant for my life. Too often we hear the Gospel for other people's lives. "I wish my husband could have heard that sermon. I wish my kids could have heard that Gospel message. I wish my parents could be here to hear this." Very few are the times when we step up to plate saying, "I am so thankful I am here so that I can change my life." We like to believe that the Gospel, its message and stories, are for other people. It was a story about a blind man, not my blindness. It was a story about a prostitute, not my own evil. It was a story about an opinionated Pharisee just like my husband.

The most beautiful aspect of our Gospel is that it is the Word of God. It has the same power to create something out of nothing. The Word of God has the same dynamism to go into regions of human life lost in hopelessness and give human dignity. The Gospel has the same mission to become incarnate in our human lives: at our supper tables, our bedrooms, our living rooms, at our barbecues and dances, in our times of birthdays and funerals, moments of graduation and sickness. The Word of God seeks its place in the temple of the human person and in the domestic church of the family. It is the food for our spiritual bodies. It rejoices at its table in our churches and longs for its place of honor in our homes: underneath the coffee table covered in dust is hardly a place of dignity. Most importantly, it longs to be lived all our lives.

Jesus taught his disciples to love as he loved. This is not a simple task. This is a life-long learning process, life-long actions. He believed in his heart that we would be the showpieces of his love to the world. He continues to risk his death and resurrection in our hands, believing eternally that we will be faithful students and practitioners of his unconditional love. He never gives up on us. It is his faith that touches our faith and, echoing the two Emmaus disciples, causes our hearts to burn with excitement at the challenge of the Gospel (Luke 24:13–35). Our starting point is not that we love God, but that he has loved us first (1 John 4:10). Our baptismal commitment to reject evil, its temptations and seductions, and to believe in God is not a credo of words but a lived response to the love of God in our life.

The call of the Gospel to live the message of Jesus is rooted in two pillars of faith: love and forgiveness. Our lives are to reflect the love and forgiveness we have received. If I have experienced the love of God in my life, then I am to love. If I have received the forgiveness of God, then I am to forgive. The blood of the cross has broken the stranglehold of the world of hate and vengeance. The Gospel desires my conversion to grace and peace that I might bring the love and forgiveness of God to the world. Fidelity to that Gospel is rooted in my understanding that I am loved by God (1 John 3:1), loved to the extreme (John 3:16), even to death on a cross (Phil 2:5–11).

The spouse's comment of desiring cancer for a moment of vengeance illustrates the depth of hurt caused in divorce. The reality, though, is that the spouse already suffers from cancer—it is the cancer of bitterness. It is eating away at the spirit and soul. It is killing the woman with hate and one-upmanship. It is a cancer desiring one last win in the issue column. It is a cancer of rage and anger. It shows poignantly the lengths one will use to get back at a spouse: even wishing one's own death to prove a point. It is easy to understand the origin and roots of the comment, but the spouse cannot see that the wish has been granted. The spouse suffers from a deadly cancer. This cancer, however, is treatable. Incredibly, it can even go into remission.

The treatments involve love and forgiveness. The spouse has to love and forgive herself. It is not the husband who is dying; it is the spouse. This person must learn how to love herself as God loves. One must love oneself whether the body is fat or thin. In God's eyes, this helpmate is the child of God. God loves this spouse unconditionally. He went to the cross for this child of his. The worth of this person was decided 2000 years ago.

The forgiveness, which is necessary for the spouse, is to forgive herself for trying to live up to unreal human expectations of what it is to love or be loved. This spouse needs to seek forgiveness for the times of not realizing the graced beauty of the Divine Image that God created. For all of the times when the spouse tried to recreate the Divine Image into the image desired by the husband, she needs to ask for forgiveness. For in all of those useless attempts, the spouse could not see or feel the love of God. This spouse had chosen a false god, the husband. The bitterness will dissipate when the spouse returns to God who created her in God's image.

The husband too suffers from the shallowness of his convictions. Does he have the capacity to love a person? Or is he in love with an image, an image of himself? The husband could never move beyond the youthful hedonism toward a mature understanding of love. For better or worse meant "so long as you are thin." Permanence is a foreign concept to the husband. He has placed conditions on the vows and in so doing has exposed the shallowness of who he is. His needs must be great. He is even too blind to recognize the shallowness of his vacationing actions. The hurts of his life are so deeply hidden that not even he can recognize them any more or be honest with himself. His self-absorption reflects the attitude that not even God can speak to his heart. The self-righteous are the most blind to the righteousness of God because they cannot distinguish in their own minds who is God (John 9:24–34).

Like the Pharisee and the publican, the husband will find it more difficult to enter into the kingdom of God until he acknowledges that he too stands in need of forgiveness (Luke 18:9–14). He needs to ask forgiveness from God for his behavior towards his spouse. He in all humility needs to ask forgiveness from his spouse for the hurt he has caused. This husband needs to seek forgiveness from God for trying to usurp God's role. He too needs the healing of the Lord that he might move beyond his selfishness and recognize that he has the capacity to love and be loved for who he is and not the image he projects.

Jesus knew who he was. He died on a cross because he would not be who others wanted him to be. He was not going to be the puppet king of nationalistic hopefuls. He was not going to be the spiritual leader of sectarian groups of Jewish assemblies, neither Pharisee nor Sadducee. He was not going to be the national Messiah of power and riches. He was not going to be restricted by his culture or his religion (John 4). He was not going to follow the prejudicial historical Zealot dictates with the enemies of his culture or religion. He was not going to follow the temple marketing practices or exclude himself from the company of prostitutes and sinners (John 2:14–17; Luke 15:1). He did not even place conditions on his forgiveness (Luke 23:39–43). He understood in the depths of his heart that his father loved him. He knew that vengeance was born of hate;

therefore, he forgave, even on the cross. He knew that all humanity, even the blind (or fat) are created in the Divine Image (John. 9:1–3); therefore, he was at peace at a tax collector's table or in the Herodian palace.

Christian relationships are born from being loved by God first. That is the root. It is the secret to any relationship succeeding. The Lord must be the reason the couple loves each other. The Lord must be the focus. The Word of God must be the first word in relating. The Word of God must be lived in the temple of the couple so that the two become truly one flesh. The couple must love and forgive each other knowing that they have been loved and forgiven by a greater love than their own. Then, they will stand before each other naked and know no shame (Gen 2:25).

PRAYER OF GRACE

I bless you Lord for your great love.
You loved me in the womb of my mother.
Your hands caressing me,
making me giggle,
You loved me;
You formed my soul.
You gave me your Divine Image.

I bless you Lord for your great love.
You gave me the beauty of your world,
Creation in its splendor.
You loved me as I walked,
As I fell,
You held me tight in my teen-age years,
and I did not even know it was you.

I bless you Lord for your great love.
You placed wonderful people in my paths
even when I went my own way.
You loved me in my strengths and fears.
You touched my soul when I was wounded;
You healed me.

I bless you Lord for your great love.
You remind me every day of your Divine Image.
It has grown with me.
It has seen your joy.
It has cried human tears.
It will embrace you in death.
I bless you Lord
for your great love.

3

My Best Friend

IVORCE IS THE SEVEREST rupture in the marriage relationship. It is a painful reminder of human failure. For the rest of a married person's life, he/she will remember the error, the blunder of life. No matter how much healing will occur, the scar of divorce will mark the married couple like the mark of Cain protected by God but cursed by men (Gen 4:15). Even if succeeding relationships occur, those relationships will always be viewed in the light of the first failed marriage. Some may even enter into subsequent relationships. If personal issues are not addressed, people may begin to number their marriages (*i.e.,* my second or third marriage). Divorce will cause both members of any former couple to question their capacity to love another human being. Throughout life, couples will ask over and over whether or not they have the simple energy to risk love once again. The prospect of divorce will remain like an unwanted guest, a haunting memory of the mistake that occurred. The residual pain and hurt, the products of any divorce, will stay in the background of the mind like a sentinel at post waiting the moment of a new relationship to strike with all the doubts and worries of entering into another flawed situation.

Divorce will always bring doubt that will tug at the mind of a person questioning his/her capacity to love again. The emotional investment, which one has placed in another human being, is incalculable. Each person has invested from a private resource of time, energy, emotion, and a wealth of human energy. Friendship, created and nurtured, has been severely cut, hacked away until it is totally unrecognizable. Each one has uttered, sometimes without ever pondering its significance, the frightening and incomprehensible commitment to love. The pledge of love has been reiterated so many times, it becomes believable to each party. Throughout the dating period, a time that couples come to know each other, each one has shown the best of faces. In longer engagements, there has been plenty

34

of time to see the whole person. Neither time nor the percentage of knowing the other human being is any guarantee that divorce will not occur. Nothing can guarantee that a marriage will survive.

In hindsight, as the pain and reality of divorce become actualized and realized, each party will question why he/she invested so much. Each spouse will state that he/she gave more, invested more, and loved more than the other spouse. As each one justifies his own participation in the marriage, each party will question his/her reserves to see if anything is left to invest in another relationship.

Do I have the capacity to love another human being? Am I emotionally capable of investing my personal savings (emotions, feelings, friendship, likes, and dislikes) in another relationship with someone who is telling me that he loves me? Didn't someone else tell me the same thing? Didn't I lose all that I had invested? Did I not do my best at loving? Naturally, these questions surface as protective measures to counter the hurt of the broken marriage, but for all of the self-preservation they generate, these questions sow seeds of self-doubt. Before divorced people enter into another relationship, they will question their capacity to love again.

Love is a word which too many couples use only to discover how elusive love really is. From the volumes of works, poems, plays, novels, music, from the endless tomes on such an enchanting emotion, love still remains an evasive platonic ideal in the mind of humanity. Everyone knows what it is and what it is not, but people still face each other with hopeless blank looks, empty vacant stares if ever asked to define love much less appropriate it. Love has two essential components: love seeks the good of another human being and works to provide for that good.

Simple common usage, however, shows the inconsistency of definition and abuse "love" has taken from our lives. Alcoholics love the bottle, and children love ice cream cones. Couples love before the altars of God but soon after find themselves loving to fight with each other. People love animals and love to stir the pot in the arguments of their families and friends. God is love, and in the most sinful inclinations and actions, people love to play God.

The difficulty and beauty of all human relationships is that human encounter blends the personalities of people. In the blending of those personalities couples enter into areas filled with the life experiences of the other person. In the dating period couples come to know the other person and begin to risk sharing the innermost parts of their personalities. They step into the territory of another human being's persona. They hear the stories of the past. They hear the jokes and review the trials each one has experienced. People become familiar with the phrases common in the other's speech. The personality of each participant begins to occupy the space of the other person. This is a beautiful moment, yet it is filled with great risks that can threaten autonomy. In this time infatuation and love can become confused.

As each party probes into the personality of the other person, emotions surface and judgments are made. Some judgments are healthy; others are not. The blending of personalities exists in a healthy atmosphere so long as each person is focused on the other. When the man or woman makes judgments as to how he/she might change the other party, he/she has begun creating the partner in his/her own image. People have to make judgments about others when they are in a relationship. This is what determines whether or not one loves the other person. A common error, however, which appears in many cases, is the domineering feeling of infatuation. Infatuation is the negation that one party may be in error about certain aspects of life. A person may actually see the flaw of the other person, but the prevailing infatuation decides to overlook the flaw. It is at this point that the initial party attributes the overlooking of the flaw to love. "He has his faults, but I love him." "She could be smarter, but I love her naiveté."

All relationships move through an infatuation period. The two personalities have to experience the other in order to decide whether or not this is the "right person for me." Problems occur when couples marry while they are still in the infatuation phase of the relationship. When they are infatuated with each other, they are moving into the other's life experiences as if it were the most natural place to be. They are completely unaware that the moment will come when they realize they have their own personalities that they have to reclaim from the other person.

Love demands the retention of one's own personality. Love is based in the individuality of the person. Christ's command, to love the Lord God with everything that we are and to love our neighbor as ourselves, has its roots in the love of self, not the love of neighbor. The love of one's neighbor has no validity if the love of self is not present (Matt 22:34–40). Love of neighbor without the love of self is as cold and impersonal as any bureaucratic welfare agency. When couples are in the infatuation stage of the relationship, love of self is difficult. When a person is so infatuated with the other person, he/she may wear different masks in order to put forward his/her best face or the face he/she thinks the other desires. Any attempt to conceal one's true personality violates the honesty with oneself that love of self requires. Couples want to show their best personality in lieu of their honest personality. Infatuation is not love. Love will always seek the good of the other person. It is more difficult than infatuation because it demands honesty.

For example: A couple is dating and one has a problem with alcohol. Infatuation will deny the problem or excuse it repeatedly. Love will demand that the problem be addressed if the relationship is to continue in a healthy manner. It is easy to understand how couples confuse infatuation with love erroneously thinking and believing that love means excusing, accepting, or ignoring the faults of another human being.

When couples begin to blend their personalities, discovering the likes and dislikes of each other, it is a time when love is required. This should be the moment when honesty is the most prevalent. This should be the time when honest judgments about one's self and the other should be made. This should be the moment when each party realizes that the other human being is an individual with his/her own likes and dislikes. It is the moment that celebrates difference. Relationships are choices made by individuals to love the differences of the other human being or to realize that the differences are so diametrical that, in all honesty, this relationship should not continue. What occurs, however, is that infatuation blurs and confuses the relationship. Being in love with love can thwart a healthy marriage. Relationships are based on two very different and complex people. They each have individual personalities that are offered to the other person. The blending of personalities is so sacred that a successful, healthy relationship will occur only when those two distinct personalities are mutually given and accepted by both members of a couple.

It is said that the most extreme of passions is really the same entity. The extreme right is only a micro-step away from being the extreme left. The most macho of men is a hair away from being gay. The circular movement of extreme passions and feelings blurs the distinctions of principles to such an extent that it becomes impossible to distinguish any uniqueness. Like the ends of a string when joined together, they find themselves being the same string. The extreme right, like the extreme left, desires the same goal: total domination at the expense of the other. The extremely

macho man finds himself in love, like the gay man, with a man—himself.
He can relate only to that which is masculine.

I remember watching two brothers at a funeral. In daily life, they
were complete opposites. One is very macho, raised to live like a man in
the Latino culture. He is a man with an incredible amount of talent, but
because of his approach to life with alcohol and other mind-influencing
drugs, he cannot harvest the talent to produce any lasting good for himself or his family. At his best, he feels sorry for himself, and at his worst,
his problems come from everyone else but him. In his house, he is the
boss. His wife and children exist to serve him. He refuses to hear any
gospel in his life or to recognize that changes are needed for the good of
the family. His alcohol abuse violates every aspect of his life, though in his
own mind, alcohol is not a problem. He views himself as the head of the
household. Although his family does not have many material things, he
has always provided for his family. He has missed every opportunity that
has been afforded him to go beyond his present situation.

The other brother is a gay man in a somewhat committed relationship. The gay brother also has an incredible amount of talent. He, however, has reaped the talent within himself and has produced a lifestyle of
comfort for himself and his partner. It has been a difficult path for this
brother in that he has had to move away from the family to a larger city.
He and his lover have gone beyond the small minds of small towns and
located themselves in a population where tolerance is practiced rather
than preached. Occupational opportunities also opened up for this brother because the city provided companies more interested in the quality
of work rather than the prejudice of where one sleeps. This gay brother
too struggles with alcohol at times but not to the extent of his straight
brother. This gay brother too has had relational difficulties, but because
the couple has had to overcome incredible societal and familial prejudice,
the couple has resolved many of their relational issues. Although there are
some systemic familial similarities, the brothers are complete opposites.
Even more so, they exemplify the extremes.

When the child of the heterosexual brother died tragically, the entire
family withdrew into the movements of grief. The father was devastated
by guilt, a debilitating emotion that can rip into the soul of any human
being. Guilt leads people into the land of "why didn't I" and "if only I
had." Death is permanent. The deceased cannot awaken to be told that the
family did love him or that they wish he were alive. The deceased cannot

rise from his casket like Lazarus no matter how many tears are shed at his tomb (John 11). The deceased cannot respond to the pleas of the living and even much less can the deceased ease the guilt of the one who should have loved him before he died.

At this point, the father began to realize how fragile life is. He also was forced to take inventory of the relationship he had with his now deceased son. No changes in behavior have occurred, and the death has provided but one more point of self-pity. Family systems, which tend to repeat the same mistakes unto the thousandth generation, moved the family to worry about the father during the days of interment. Remember that a Latino family goes beyond the immediate family to include cousins, aunts, uncles, and at times even the closest of friends referred to as *compadres*.

Because the plan of God is immersed in God's divine love, it happened that the gay brother was the deceased young man's godfather. Coming from a large immediate Latino family, the pairing of siblings can be confusing as time and situations compound the relationships. Both of these two men are strong in their views of life. There is no compromise on issues. Each one is at peace with live and let live, but the only social contact they share is within a family setting. There is no animosity between the brothers. It is very clear, however, who is right and who is wrong on certain moral issues.

Everyone seems to understand the boundaries and limits on issues and certainly is attuned to what can be addressed. Homosexuality is never broached in any family setting. Whereas it may be totally acceptable for the straight brother to hug or kiss his wife, it is totally unacceptable for the gay brother to do the same to his partner. The family has learned to operate in this manner. As the funeral mass took place, by the divine plan of God, it happened that the father sat between his wife and his gay brother.

The beauty of the service drew the congregation into the liturgy of resurrection. Every heartstring was pulled, and every human sense was gently stroked so that God would be praised even in death. Then it happened. God, who is love, manifested himself. Without them knowing it, the love of God enveloped the two men. These two very different men bound together by tragedy were bound together in emotions. With the grace of tears, they clung to the only one who could feel as they felt: each other. I watched as the left became the right and the right ceded any claims to authority, as the yellow sun submerged into the blue water producing the green horizon. I saw two men hug and cry as no two men could share. I could see the Christ in one reaching out to the Christ in the other. I could hear St. Paul preaching the oneness of Christ: no Jew, no Greek; no male, no female; no label, no categories (see Col 3:11). It was the prodigal brothers rejoicing at the same party (Luke 15:11-32 or does the older brother enter after his father's pleading?). It was painful. The passion and death of an innocent young man was healing two very grown men. The tears and the embracing continued in God's eternal time as each man reached into the depth of the other's soul and loved him for who he was and not for anything else. They were brothers. In that pain of death, they had found the only person who suffered with the same intensity. In their circular movement of extreme principles and passions, they had become one. Their embrace born out of great emotional pain produced the overpowering awesome witness of love. God had won as they became one in him. In a moment of incredible grief, they were graced.

That point where east meets west, where the extremes touch, is a very emotional and tender moment reserved to the Almighty. As often as humanity trespasses into that region of the blurring of opposites without being spiritually prepared for the experience, it runs the risk of looking upon the face of God and dying. It is the moment when the lion lies with the calf and the wolf dwells with the lamb. It is the time when the child plays with the adder, the infant next to the den of the cobra (Isa 11:6–8). It is the graced moment when lion and lamb, both delicate animals created by the tenderness of the fingers of God, frolic in the peace of Eden.

That particular area of unity is so fragile and sensitive that one can hear the command of God to remove your shoes for you are on holy ground (Exod 3:5). One wrong movement, one wrong shift of thought back into oneself and not the other person, will rupture the experience. To live and move and have one's being in the delicate moment of the blending of the extremes is to lose oneself into the totality of the other. It is not to think of oneself (1 Cor 13). It is a delicate balance to live in the moment of extremes. It is even a more delicate dance when love is involved. Relationships hang in the tension of love and hate. As those two extreme ends touch, one wrong shift in thought or word and love becomes hate.

Divorce is the human experience where an error occurred in the marital relationship as the two extremes in personalities touched without being spiritually prepared. Divorce is the reality that the lion ate the lamb and the adder bit the child. Divorce is the experience that the marriage looked upon the face of God and died because God had ceased to be the focus of the life of the couple. Divorce is the truth that humanity did not know how to love much less understand its requirements. It is the rupture of relationship among God, husband, and wife. Divorce is the constant hurting reminder that people did not seek the good of the other person and that they did not work to provide for that good. Divorce is the flag waving in the wind for all to see that couples sought their own good rather than the good of the spouse. Divorce is the painful lived experience of broken friendship.

At the core of divorce lies the most painful question that few people address honestly with anyone: Am I lovable? Divorce is a rejection of a human being. Like a two-edged sword, it slices both parties in one-way or another. The greatest hurt arises from the individual desiring to know "what was so repugnant in me that I cannot be loved." It is the greatest hurt because the divorced person struggles within his/her own mind with very personal issues and questions. The divorced person seeks an answer about self and yet does not have the capacity at this moment to hear any response which will satisfy the needs caused by the separation. The rupture is so severe as to cause tremendous self-doubt within both individuals.

When divorce occurs, it causes a person to question his or her own self-worth. If a husband repeatedly tells his wife how worthless and stupid she is, she may be able to fend off his verbal and emotional abuse for years. The meticulous and repeated hate, however, will slowly weave its way into the life of the wife. Evil has a way of picking at a wound until it bleeds or someone finds a cure (John 8:7). The day will come when she will pose the question to herself. The day she questions her worth will be the saddest day of her life, for she will have handed her life over to the warped machinations of another human being. The minute she questions her worth as wife, or mother, or human being, the abuser has won. The husband no longer has to be present to abuse his spouse. She will do that on her own. When divorce occurs, a person relives in her mind all of the accusations which have been leveled against her.

Divorce demands that love come into question. The court is convened in the mind as words and memories are placed on trial. Emotions and feelings are called as witnesses. Even the spectators in the mental courtroom are cross-examined as if to find any justification for what has occurred. Behind all of the mental drama, the question will still remain. Am I lovable? It is no longer a simple question of whether or not I have the capacity to love another human being. Now it is a deeper and more frightening question of whether or not I love me. Do I have the emotional resources to love myself? Any divorced person will search his soul in honesty and self-pity trying to find the answer. Divorce has told him that there is a flaw in how he relates to people. It has exposed his inability to love for better or worse. Divorce tells the rest of the world that at least one person on this earth does not desire to live with him or her. In severe and cruel situations, divorce even demands that any claims to friendship be ceded. Divorce sets off the alarm that something is askew in the personality of both husband and wife. Can he look at his life honestly and identify the positive areas of his life and call into question those areas that cry for change? Can she acknowledge complicity in the failed marriage?

Love of self is an arduous task of continued self-examination and honesty. It demands the truthful discernment and introspection of one's life. It requires the human acknowledgment that some things are not in "my" control. An honest love of self will require that each person recognize his/her dependence on the Creator. Love of self is a daily reflection of personal decisions, behaviors, and judgments to make sure life has been lived by what God desires.

When divorce occurs, it renders a person so emotionally drained that love of self is nearly impossible. People get stuck in the endless barrage of hate hurled from the other party that blinds them to seeing and correcting honestly their own flaws. Even when the other party is not present, one will hear the accusations over and over in one's mind. The mind will defend itself from any utterances it hears from the other party. It will deafen itself to anything said from the mouth of the previous lover. Before any self-love can occur, a person must lick his wound of being told by his spouse that at best he is worthless. He must now ask if what has been said of him is true. His tears come from self-doubt, self-questioning of what it is within himself or herself that the other party finds repulsive.

The rejection is so severe that a former husband may even question whether or not he loves himself. Love of self is difficult and requires the prayerful discernment of truth. When someone is going through a divorce, love of self is even more difficult because one's energies are spent in self-defense, self-justification, and at times self-righteousness. There is no opportunity to reflect honestly about oneself because the other party may use it to her advantage. Love of self admits to vulnerability within oneself. It is not self-pity. Love of self is the acknowledgment that God came to save the sinful. Love of self admits to the positive and negative areas of a life.

Love of self is the personal realization that one always stands in need of the mercy of God. Love of self is the realization that one's life is so graced by the presence of God that one builds the kingdom of God by living his Gospel. As one prayerfully questions the positive and negative areas of one's life, love of self is the honest and graced negation of egotism and false humility in one's life. Love of self is the permission one gives to oneself to be vulnerable with oneself, one's feelings, one's graces, one's sins. Love of self allows a person to see oneself naked in the garden and not be afraid of what God has already seen (Gen 3:8–11a).

In divorce situations, love of self is extremely difficult because, if honestly addressed, a divorced person may realize some truth to what a spouse is saying. An honest love of self may uncover a truth about himself or herself which he or she did not want to see. Because divorce renders a person so tender to the moment, he/she will quickly move from love of self to an exaggeration of the uncovered truth. Love of self is difficult because it requires looking at the total person and not just one aspect. In a divorce situation, any honest uncovered truth would force one to state that the other party was correct about a flaw. Rather than seeing a total picture of life, its graces and sins, the reality of divorce would focus and concentrate upon the flaw which is honestly uncovered. Any spouse would be forced to realize that perhaps what his spouse had told him, in all anger and hate, was true.

The mind and emotions at this stage cannot comprehend that any truth could possibly come from someone who has hurt his feelings so grievously. The wife has broken his heart. The spouse has taken the most precious pearl that he could offer (his entire being) and thrown it into a pile of dung. Love of self cannot be achieved because divorce with its net of hate and retaliation has caused him to focus on self-defense and self-pity.

Self-defense and self-pity, when combined, produce the ingredients of depression. All depression renders one unhealthy. Depression is the blindness that cannot see the Divine Image. Depression is the deafness that cannot hear the whisper of God calling one's name. Depression is the "after it's all said and done, I don't even love me." Depression is the rejection of life, the choosing of death. Depression has gathered all negative moments and placed them in the mind of an individual with such a force that a person believes he/she is worthless. Depression denies any goodness. It rejects the beauty of friendships. It blocks any thought of grace. Depression is the moment when the Holy Spirit must intercede for us because we cannot pray ourselves (Rom 8:26–27). Like all illness, depression cries for healing. Depression after a divorce is devastating. It leaves a spouse fighting invisible ghosts and arguing mentally with no one. Depression attacks at unsuspecting moments, laughing as it dredges up old memories, good and bad ones, forcing the tears of loneliness to come down like rain. Without any notice, one is placed again in the situation of a memory, forced to relive the questioning and eventually the hurt.

The depression of divorce affects the work place, the home, and even recreational moments. The depression of divorce affects all human contact as the divorced person seeks anyone who will listen to his or her cause. The depression of divorce will re-evaluate every friendship with harsh consequences in the aftermath. The depression of divorce echoes the overwhelming sadness of the Psalms as one cries to a deaf and uncaring God: my only friend is darkness (Ps 88).

Depression produces the tears of failure in one's life. It unmasks all strengths and strips people of all human dignity. Friends and family will continually make matters worse as they question what went wrong in the marriage relationship. The divorced person will ask himself that question over and over. He will receive as many different answers as the number of times he questions himself. In marriages of lengthier periods, the questions and answers are magnified. The divorced person will look to his friends for answers seeking a balm which no one possesses. The friend who held the answer, who knows where the balm is hidden, is the one who has rejected him in the divorce.

CASE STUDY

The couple had a quite lengthy relationship. Each one had relationships before meeting each other. They dated approximately four years before marrying. There was a significant moment in their dating when the young man mentioned to his fiancée that Javier was his best friend. He was serious. He had known Javier before his fiancée. They had shared many moments of friendship before the fiancée ever came into the picture. They had shared their hopes and dreams. They had told each other their fantasies. They had partied together. They were good drinking buddies. They had been the counselors for each other as each one dated different people. They were the confidants. They had fought with each other, spilling margaritas on each other, and demanding that one live up to the principles of the other. They spoke of their likes and dislikes frequently. They even meddled into the romantic affairs of the other trying to determine who should date whom. What they held in common was their faith in each other. They wanted the good for the other person and worked to provide that good. Javier and the young man had even spotted the fiancée from afar and had commented to each other what they desired.

The jealousy never came from Javier. He was very sure of his friendship with the young man. He was his best friend. The fiancée, however, had moments of jealousy. Too much time was spent with Javier. Too many things were held in confidence with Javier and not with her. The fiancée, leery of Javier from the beginning, even had sex with him. It did not matter to the young man. Javier was his best friend; the fiancée was his fiancée. When the young man mentioned to the fiancée that Javier was his best friend, the fiancée could not cope with that reality. To be a spouse meant that spouses were best friends. The young man tried desperately to explain the concept of friendship and spouses as he understood it, but he made no progress with the fiancée. Spouses were supposed to be best friends. In a moment of frustration, the young man ceded the argument by trying to prove his love for his fiancée. The fiancée would be his best friend. He lied to himself. He knew in his heart and so did Javier, that Javier was his best friend. Javier said nothing. The label of "best friend" is either lived or a label. The fiancée could have the label. Javier would continue living the part.

As the couple went through college, one of the professors became enamored with the fiancée. The professor actively sought out the fiancée. He was kind to the young man, but the hidden agenda was to have an active relationship with the fiancée. The professor found moments when the two of them would spend time together. The seeds he planted took root when the professor convinced the couple to have sex with him. The professor desired the fiancée and included the young man because it was the only way this relationship would occur.

The young man knew that night that this professor was sexually immature. He knew that night as he saw the professor have sex with his fiancée that he would never be a friend of theirs. The next day the professor continued his conquest scheme telling the fiancée how guilty he felt about the episode. He really wasn't like that. He didn't sleep with his students.

The fiancée and the young man discussed the episode. He stated strongly his opposition to this professor. He related his concerns about the hypocrisy of the professor. He knew and stated that this professor did not want their own right relationship to grow or succeed. The fiancée listened but determined it was probably more jealousy than fact coming from the young man. The couple decided to put distance between themselves and the professor. The professor did not relent. He pursued the fiancée through educational opportunities. Although nothing sexual occurred again, it was obvious that this professor desired the love of the fiancée.

As the couple married, the professor still pursued the young spouse. The young man made it very clear he felt in his heart that this professor did not want their marriage to succeed. The spouse said to the husband that the professor was not just an educator but also now a close friend. The spouse felt sorry for the professor's confusion about his life. Javier's name was thrown around every now and then as a defense mechanism. The young man replied from the depth of his heart that he hated the professor. He wanted his spouse to understand that point. In the young man's mind, if his spouse understood that he hated this professor, then she should not have any type of relationship or friendship with him. Hate is a strong emotion and word, but it was very clear to the couple that the young man hated the professor. He did not like any contact at all with the professor. He was a snake whose ego was bigger than the campus where he taught.

On one social occasion, the couple came to a party early. They began drinking early that night. The husband drank a dark ale to which he was not accustomed. It went straight to his senses. He was always a mean drunk. He could be very mean in life itself, but his drinking heightened every experience. He would become abusive at the drop of a hat. Once he threatened a man on crutches offering to break his other leg. As the party wore on, it happened that the professor was also a guest. The couple had known that beforehand but had come to an agreement to be at peace. They loved each other.

The couple sat on the couch. The professor plopped himself on an opposite chair. He was proclaiming his self-worth, flaunting his knowledge, masking his insecurities, and flirting openly with the spouse. The young man was enraged. The alcohol burned within him. He shared his feelings with his spouse later.

"I wanted to break the bottle on the table and ram it up his ass. I wanted to punch him in the face and kick his groin for the filthy asshole he is."

The professor could sense the anger from the young man so he directed a nonsensical question to the young man. He asked twice because no response came. The young man loved his spouse. He had vowed not to interrupt this important gathering for his spouse. After a frightening gaze into the depths of hell, he rose from the couch and went into the restroom never answering or acknowledging his enemy. He hated this man for the simple reason that the professor never wanted the couple's marriage to succeed. To this day, after a painful divorce, with each one living separate lives, he hates that professor. The professor is still the friend of the spouse. There is speculation of a sexual nature though nothing can be proven.

The next day the spouse commented to the husband about the scene.

I wish you could have seen your face when the professor was talking with you. I thought you were going to go over and beat the hell out of him.

I hate that man.

He is my friend and has helped me greatly in my career.

So that he can sleep with you!

Do you think that little of me?

I hate that man because he does not want us to succeed.

I thought you were going to hit him.

I should have. I should have cut his dick off.

Why do you hate him so much?

Because you can't see what he is doing.

I love you. He's accepted that.

I hate him.

This couple could be the most loving and the most hateful to each other. At times, it seemed to others that they loved to live in the extremes of love and hate. When they loved, they loved to the utmost. When they hated, it was a war zone. As they defined for themselves their lives, their problems in relating to one another mounted. The husband always blamed the influence of the professor on his spouse for their marital difficulties. Like Rome's Carthage, he was the enemy to be destroyed.

At breakfast one morning, the husband told his spouse, "I love you." It had been a hellacious night of arguing. The spouse acknowledged the statement and retorted, "Yes, but do you like me?" In a moment of honest friendship the now older man replied in the negative.

"I do not like the way you treat me. I do not like the way you speak to me. You treat me with little kindness. You do not respect me as a husband. Even your family with all of their prejudices is at least kind to me. You are not even kind to me. I do not like your insensitivity to my feelings. You say you love me but do nothing that shows me love. You make me feel as if I am a burden to you. No, I do not like you or your behavior with me in public much less in private."

After many years of marriage, the couple divorced. The extremes of their personalities had crossed into the area reserved for the Almighty. They were not spiritually prepared to seek the good of the other person. When asked, each blames the other or looks to various reasons for the separation. The inner rage of the husband has never subsided. His self-righteousness continues to consume him. Divorce has taken away any semblance of peace within his life. On a recent vacation, the husband, when he was sober and when he was drunk, told Javier that he was his best friend. He had always been his best friend. Javier smiled. He knew that many years ago.

PASTORAL REFLECTION

Friendship is a costly ingredient in relationships. People generally move in circles of friends and acquaintances. Even friends are stratified and classified as to how they relate to an individual: good friend vs. close friend; close friend vs. best friend. Couples entering into marriage usually enter into the relationship believing the spouse will be the best friend. It is not always the case. Married couples have friends as a couple. Each spouse, however, may have his own personal friends. The intermingling of these friendships may take its toll on a marriage.

Healthy marriages will speak of the relationship between the spouses as one of being best friends. They share with each other. They work together for the good of the home. They do not keep secrets. They are proud that secrets are shared with each other. They address problems and worries together. They draw their strength from each other. Because they are best friends with each other (truly best friends), they are kind and honest to one another. They will also have their moments of anger and frustration with each other. There may be the possible moments of distancing from each other until they realize what the other person means to him in his life.

Healthy marriages are those that have moved beyond infatuation and have chosen to live in the realm of love. It is a choice made by both parties for the quality of honesty in their relationship. They have crossed into the personalities of each other and have decided to be at peace with likes and dislikes. They are not afraid of the truths that must be faced in their lives. Excusing the faults of the other has decreased greatly as they have found the fruits of honesty rooted in love. Each one has discovered the key of loving one's self so as to be able to love the other person.

Jesus' interpretation of the Mosaic Law roots itself in a triangular dependence of persons (Matt 22:33–40). Love of God is worthless if it is not manifested in the love of neighbor which is useless if it is not based in love of self. Jesus is the prime example of love. He desired the best for us and gave his life for us. His is divine love, but it is not beyond our grasp. He is the example that we emulate. In his love for us he does not excuse our faults. He challenges us, however, to go beyond our errors (John 21:15–17). He loves us greatly in that he is not afraid to show us the truth within our lives. He wears no mask as he confronts our personality. He hides nothing as he looks into our individuality. In his eternal patience, he provides all the means for our total conversion to him.

Healthy marriages recognize the beauty of the individuality of the other person. They grow in the graced moments of life and challenge each other to move beyond any sinfulness. Healthy marriages are those which live the triangular love daily constantly hearing the voice of the Eternal Lover in their marriage, gracing them at every moment and challenging them to move beyond themselves as a couple.

There are other healthy marriages in which one or both of the spouses may have best friends who are not the spouse. Couples have to determine between themselves how those friendships will affect the marriage. They have to determine the limits and boundaries of interference from those friendships. It is a delicate balance which has to be maintained. One of the determining factors in evaluating these friendships is to measure how much the best friend wants the marriage to succeed.

It is impossible to ask any fiancé or fiancée to have a friendship with another human being on the same level that exists between the original best friends. It is not impossible, however, to measure by word and deed how much that best friend wants the marriage to be healthy. There are best friends with other agendas. With smiling faces, these "best" friends can work against the marriage of their best friend. Sometimes from the very inception of the relationship, they actively work against the couple. They never wanted the marriage to succeed at all.

Struggling with their marriage vows, couples search for advice. They look to ones whom they can trust. Best friends, who are not the spouse, all too often provide answers too readily based on the friendship without any discernment. Spouses, struggling in their marriages without realizing their own vulnerability of the moment, can overlook the bias of the best friend, as divorce becomes a greater option. Because the pain of the marriage is so great, one fails to measure how much the best friend wanted and worked for the success of the marriage.

In their infatuation with each other, this couple chose to lie to themselves rather than face their feelings honestly. As they were living in the personality territory of the other, they should have taken a broader inventory. Neither one chose to love himself. The husband chose a lie by stating that his fiancée was his best friend. The fiancée chose a lie by demanding change from the future husband. This simple dishonest part of the relationship affected the entire marriage. In a blind misunderstanding of love, they at that early stage of the relationship chose to excuse the faults of each other thus condemning themselves to a marriage based on dishonesty at many different subsequent levels.

It is too easy to blame Javier or the professor. The responsibility lies with the couple not being honest with each other's personalities from the beginning. They had closed their eyes to the reality of who the other person really was. In their infatuation with each other, they excluded love. The pain of that exclusion is that even their friendship to this day is non-existent. Neither one of them loved himself enough to recognize his error in the exercise of the relationship. If they could not love themselves, then how was it ever possible to say that they loved each other?

Jesus, in the Gospel of John in a very moving discourse to his beloved disciples, makes a most challenging statement to them before he dies. He tells them that they are no longer servants of his. He changes the relationship that they have with him stating that now they are his friends. He reminds them that friendship is relational. They are his friends if they do as he asks: to love another as he has loved (John 15:12–15).

Jesus' teaching on love is not impossible, but it is the most challenging part of the Gospel. He desires we respond to him as friends willing to live as he lived, capable of loving as he loved. He believes we have the capacity to walk into the personality of another human being and bring peace just as he has done with us. He believes that we will carry the Gospel of unconditional love so that the world might see in us his resurrected presence (John 13:35). He knew that his friends would have to be more than followers or students. He expects us to be the leaders, the practitioners of his commandment. He is our best friend, for he chooses to love our graced moments and challenge us to go beyond the sinfulness of our lives. He, who is the Way, desires our love based in Truth, so that the world might have Life (John 14:6a). When the commandment to love as he loves is practiced by his friends, then there truly is life in abundance (John 10:10).

A PRAYER OF FRIENDSHIP

Lord, in every moment of my life
You have walked.
I felt your presence.
I heard your voice.
You were creator and I, a creature.
You were God and I, a human being.
You were the just judge and I, the penitent.
You were the shepherd and I, the sheep.
You, the teacher,
I, the disciple.

Lord in every moment of my life,
You have walked,
You, the Savior
I, the sinner.
I sit at your table.
You the Bread of Life
and only by your grace,
You call me friend.

4

La Madrugada

Divorce elicits an emotional embarrassment. This embarrassment is a constant reminder of human frailty. The human emotions surface all at once and create a cacophony of confusion at such intensity that any human being is left devastated and exhausted in trying to put life back into order. Divorce is the town crier reminding all the participants and anyone who comes into contact with the divorce that something has come in between the professed public love of two people. Emotionally, divorce never leaves anyone with a clean slate. Divorce is the mark of failure in the idealized world of societal marriage morés. Even when divorce is the result of a good decision, like leaving an abusive marriage, it scars the human memory for life.

Marriage created an illusion in a public forum that two human beings would live for better or worse, richer or poorer, in sickness and health. Marriage stated that only death would be the cause of any separation. Each participant in the marriage entered into the union with a clear knowledge of the vows. In their moments of love for each other, each one had already professed these ideal concepts though they may not have realized what the vows entailed. By the time any couple stands before any priest, minister, or judge, they have already entertained the idea of marriage and what it means to them. Their pre-conceptions and understanding of marriage have been formed by their families, friends, and, more often than not, a media saturated with fairy-tale illusions. By the time the church is reserved for any wedding, most couples have already made up their minds about the "do's and don'ts" of marriage. They have all the answers and have determined that they will not commit the same mistakes other couples have.

Others, because of the prevalent divorce mentality currently in the United States culture, enter into marriage with the idea that if the marriage does not work, then divorce is always an option. Divorce is not going to happen to them, but in case it does, it won't be any "big deal" since so many other people have been divorced. Since their minds are already formed about marriage, any required pre-marital preparation is just that, *required*. Couples usually expend more energy in planning their wedding than in planning their marriage.

Pre-marital preparation by any denomination battles with couples who have come to the preparation with their minds already programmed as to how they will live marriage. Pre-marital preparation must compete with caterers, bands, invitations, photographers, florists, hall rentals, tuxedos, bridesmaids' dresses, unity candles, wedding coordinators, limousines, junior bridesmaids and groomsmen (whatever those are), future in-laws' opinions, rings and things.

Most couples do not come to pre-marital preparation of their own free will. They attend the preparation because the classes are required if the marriage is to take place in a religious setting. By now it is common knowledge that most mainline denominations require some type of pre-marital counseling. It is also common knowledge that most couples attend reluctantly out of duty.

Attendance is seen as a hoop through which the couple must jump in order to get to the side of marriage. Couples attend either with a bias that no one is going to tell them how to live their marriage or with complacency that masks ambivalence. It is always easier to minister to those with a bias than with the complacent who refuse to be challenged or dare to challenge. Pre-marital preparation acknowledges that marriage is work. Marriage preparation requires work from both parties to anticipate the practice of their vows.

Couples marrying before a civil magistrate have no pre-marital preparation. They enter into marriage to legalize a union based on their love for each other. Since there is no perfect example of marriage, their marriage, in their mind, is the one that will last forever. Their marriage is the one which will be the example for all of the rest. Pre-marital preparation is a foreign concept and certainly no guarantee of a successful marriage. Couples marrying before a civil magistrate and even those with a religious ceremony sometimes fail to understand that pre-marital preparations are the tools to be used, to be put into practice, not a magic answer to create a perfect marriage. If the marriage ends with divorce, it is more than likely that the means (communication, honesty, trust, unity, fidelity, etc.) have been neglected for an end.

The simple vows of having and holding from this day forward do not explicate the intricacies of married life: shared space, food, bills, home, children, and spiritual life. The vows do not tell of the moments of disagreement or frustration. The vows do not envision the moments of non-communication or un-communicated expectations. The vows do not speak of the times of routine or ennui, the times of hurt feelings or angst. The vows cannot imagine the moments of loneliness or the seeking of outside pleasures. The vows have no concept of lay-offs or intricate and often impossible work schedules. The vows cannot envision human tiredness or anger or the toll they take on the human person. Vows do not speak of the work a marriage requires.

I recall speaking with a couple who liked to talk about "the work of marriage." The married couple were of mixed races. One spouse was of German ancestry and the other was Latino. They liked to talk about how their marriage worked. Knowing and having lived the difficulty of a marriage with two very distinct cultural realities complicating their vows, they would generally speak of their reality in terms of how it was possible.

In speaking about inter-cultural, inter-racial marriages, the spouse of German ancestry would always remark that these types of marriages "could work." The spouse of Latino ancestry would retort that mixed marriages "take a lot of work." It is a simple nuance but speaks volumes about how the two viewed the marriage relationship. This couple was officially married for thirteen years, three months, and thirty days. Evidently the required work was not put into practice by both in equal measures.

Divorce is the clearest example of the lack of knowledge about the work marriage requires. It indicates that a couple or at least one of the parties did not have the capacity to understand what marriage demands. Divorce terminates a marriage. It does not seek to lay blame on either party. Any couple will attack each other with blame all by themselves. Conditions included in a divorce decree are an attempt at justice and equity not an indication of who is better or worse as a spouse.

As couples become enmeshed in the complications of divorce trials and legalese, they lose sight of the reasons why the divorce occurred. Blaming resurrects old issues and memories. More often than not as a divorce progresses, couples seek one more chance to gain the upper-hand in a fast deteriorating situation. In the public forum of marriage, the couple professed their undying love for each other. In the public forum of divorce, couples profess their dying love for each other. The publicity produces the emotional embarrassment.

When the couple entered into marriage, they announced it to all of their friends. In some cases, the wedding was a big production including family members no one has seen since the last big family production and will not see again until the next production. The civil license proclaims the public unity even to the uninvited. This publicity is one of great joy. The publicity, however, renders the marriage open to public scrutiny of life. Marriage is a public reality. Since its inception, marriage is under a magnifying glass telling the world about successful relationships. Because of publicity, marriage invites the critique of everyone—family, friends, and acquaintances.

At different weddings, I have heard the guests belittle the relationship of the bride and groom as they feasted on the wedding dinner and drank the free alcohol. People are quick to judge everything in the wedding. By the time the ceremony, reception, or dinner are finished, guests have had their fill and taste of everything significant to the bride and groom. In their gossip, they have even eaten the newlyweds. Although their comments may seem like gossip and rumors, they are but the tip of the iceberg of what the couple will face in their married life. Private marriage does not exist.

When the public marriage fails, a public divorce occurs. It is the forum where previous lovers expose the secrets of their private lives. Herein lies one of the difficulties in a marriage situation. Although marriage is a very public state, its lived experience is both a public and private reality. In the privacy of their home couples live a private life, but in society, their unity is public. The combination of the public and the private often leads to disunity.

Divorce exposes the disunity for all to see. It allows the public to examine the private reality of the couple. What was shared in secret, what was held in trust, what was not intended for the public domain, is brought now before a public forum with outsiders peering in and offering unwanted judgments. The initial criticism of the wedding creeps back into the story of the couple's life. Gossip and rumor resurrect themselves without any concern for the feelings or privacy of the couple. To an even greater extent, the public now becomes aware of the moments of very private pain and anguish.

The great joy and public announcement of love magnifies the sadness and public announcement of anger, sometimes to the point of hate. Divorce allows for every private secret to be broadcast, aired before anticipating families as if the pain of someone else eases their own pain. The details of why and what happened are never sufficient for the demand from friends and families. Everyone looks to assign blame in some manner or other.

Families and friends usually discard the pain of those going through the divorce. Families do not understand that they are privileged to know the private lives of individuals. They hear rumors and allegations from odd sources. Without any concern for the privacy of the husband or wife, they make judgments about the marriage and its failure and are quick to make their opinions known to the divorcing relative. Family members and friends offer their opinions even when their opinions are not sought. The divorced person is suffering a loss. He/she is grieving. Opinions and judgments very rarely address the loss. Opinions usually look to blame one or both of the individuals or to speak ill of the relationship.

When families and friends do not address the loss in an encouraging way, the pain of the loss remains with the individual. His or her private life has been exposed for all to see. His or her secret intimacies have been left open to ridicule by strangers and people close to him or her. Because divorce is a public action, anyone has access to the divorce decrees which detail everything from property to children to debt. The divorced person is tried not only in civil court but in the court of public opinion as well.

The divorce phenomenon basically follows the same pattern as the marriage. The wedding is public, and then the marriage moves into a period of comparative privacy. The couple alone has to determine how the marriage will be lived. The public formalities of the wedding have ceased, and the couple is left with the marriage to be worked out between themselves.

Divorce follows the same pattern. There is an ugly public formality of the divorce action with families and friends stating their opinions of shock and dismay, but then the divorced persons are left alone to work out the consequences. Many times those consequences begin with nurturing the feelings of loss within their life. The surfacing of so many feelings (anger, rage, grief) all at once can overwhelm the person taking him or her to the innermost regions of depression. Hearing the pain makes one cry.

At times, family and friends, not knowing how to reach the hurt individual, attempt to move the person beyond the immediate crisis situation. They generally want the divorced person to "get over it and get on with life." Family and friends are unconscious of the grieving needs of the divorced person. They do not understand that grieving is for more than just a day, and it is not limited to time or space. Time is no guarantee of a total healing or that grieving has ceased.

In the grieving mode the divorced person must face the horrors of personal embarrassment. Although everyone else may not see the situation as a "big deal," the divorced sees his/her entire life played over on a gigantic screen in the mind. They relive every moment in search of some personal dignity. In their minds, they look upon the face of hell only to realize it was a hell that they as a couple created. The mistakes of marriage become magnified and exaggerated.

In those exaggerations the divorced person faces the shame of his life fearing that all can see what he sees. It is a sensation of falling into the ground and seeing layer upon layer of one's self peeling away like an onion. The mouth opens to scream as the fall begins, but no noise comes forth, though the scream is deafening. As one falls deeper and deeper into the self, accompanied by that deafening "no sound," the soul screams for someone to catch him so as not to lose one's mind. The ex-spouse can feel the layers of self falling from him with the rush of wind as the grieving "ex" falls deeper into the abyss of grief. At the end of the fall is the realization of a person left alone. No longer is there a question of another human being capable of living "with me." Now comes the reality of "can I live with me?"

Divorce highlights the mistakes of life big or small and glosses over the positive areas of selflessness in marriage. Divorce evokes personal feelings of people even after many years. They will speak of that moment of their life as if it happened yesterday. The memories seem dormant, but as reflection occurs, the mind is quick to recall the events and situations that elicited great pain as motivating factors of the divorce to come. Even when people are in new relationships, the mention of the previous divorce projects the divorced person back into a reality thought buried or healed recalling old wounds. The wound may not hurt as much, but the scar of divorce is still very real. If the scar is picked enough, like any physical wound, it will fester or bleed. Divorce does not equal good times.

Divorce focuses only on the tragic moments of the marriage. It cannot imagine that good times possibly existed. Focusing solely on the separation of the union and its consequences, if the marriage had any good times, they are clouded and shelved to the memory of non-existence. Because of the feelings of sadness, good times (which would have had to occur at sometime in the marriage) are overlooked, not mentioned, and hold no value in the divorce, even in its future memory.

Embarrassment focuses on un-answerable questions. What happened? Why was I so stupid? Why couldn't I see it coming? Why did I stay in the marriage for so long? What is it about me that he doesn't like? Why did he do this? What about all of the time I have been in this relationship? Why is this happening to me? Will we ever get back together? What if I change? What about the kids? What about all of those love letters? Will I ever get over this? Who will ever love me? Should I try to hold onto this person? Should I try to win him back? Do I want him back? Did he ever mean it when he said that he loved me? Were there no good times at all? Am I that repulsive? Is there nothing about me he appreciates? Was there never a moment of true love? Is he hurting as I am hurting? Does he not feel the same pain I feel? When will I stop crying? How do I tell my family? Does anyone care about me? All those years lost? Will I ever see the sun again? Is it not the same moon shining on the both of us?

These and similar questions probe the human psyche to no good end. They are the questions to which one will always return when the broken marriage is recalled. No matter how many times these questions are asked, and no matter what is the span of time when the questions are asked, there will never be a sufficient answer. They are rhetorical questions. All of these questions are based in a relationship involving two different people. Although there is no sufficient answer, they sting with the same intensity.

It is evident that healing has to occur, but there is no correct way to heal or a definite amount of time which guarantees that the healing process has been completed. Healing involves addressing the rage and anger, and disappointment—not an easy process especially if the marriage has been a long one.

In longer marriages, a couple has grown up together. They have experienced life together. They have formed many of their opinions and beliefs filtered through the eyes and thoughts of another human being, one whom they trusted with the private secrets of their heart. In longer marriages, a couple has shared too many intimate aspects of their lives, blending their individualities at times in many non-productive ways. This is the person with whom they have had sex. This is the person who knows the intimacy of their sexual behavior. This is the person with whom they have risked their nakedness, the physical, the emotional, and the spiritual (Gen 2:25). A couple divorcing from a long-term marriage experiences having to rediscover who they are as individuals in all facets of life (Gen 3:10).

The emotions in that process of self-rediscovery are overwhelming. As an ex-spouse tries to identify his/her own personality. The "ex" makes every attempt to divorce from what he/she learned from the other spouse. If there is anger (and there always is), the behavior can become violent toward self or others. Pictures are torn in an attempt (unsuccessful but definitive) to eradicate the memory of the other person. Wineglasses are broken. Items and gifts are smashed. Letters and cards are cursed, burned, or returned vindictively. The Almighty is called upon to un-create the other individual. Tears and screaming fill empty rooms as a person cries for vengeance for being devastated by a broken marriage.

These and similar actions are the expressions of trying to annihilate the memory of another human being. These violent actions are in all reality the desire of one party to hurt the other. It is not the glass that is being broken. The glass represents the ex-spouse. May he be shattered! May his life be broken into irreparable pieces! May his soul rot! The self-rediscovery, mired in anger and pain, draws a wicked strength in the desire that another human being be purged, expunged. This is not a road to a healthy self-rediscovery, yet it occurs more often than not. It does not cease either in a certain time or space. It is not a one-time feeling. Angry-or hate-filled rediscovery lacks the grace of God to heal properly.

On an emotional level, the same divorce process takes place. Things that their partner held sacred are trashed. Moments, which a partner found comical or interesting, are ridiculed as stupid or moronic. The times that the partner viewed as loving and tender are now portrayed as hypocritical or based on lies. If those moments were tender and loving, then why is the divorce occurring? The memories or events, which the partner cherished emotionally, are now scorned. Longer marriages have an ample supply of emotional material to negate, destroy, or mutilate.

Sadly though, people seeking a personal rediscovery coming out of a long-term relationship have a more difficult time at healing because of the emotional baggage of many years. The majority of one's life was spent in learning about life with the person whom he/she now hates. Growing up together, the couple enjoyed a friendship that has now ended. The reality of growing up together and learning about life (finances, love, relationship, sharing, friendship) comes crashing down as both husband and wife now have to figure out life without the other person who helped formulate the marriage vision. Some spouses have identified so much with each other that now as divorce becomes the reality, they will state that they do not know how to be themselves, for in their own mind, they have always seen themselves as part of another human being's life. They have lost a sure sense of their individuality.

Individuality should be the focus of rediscovery instead of hate. Every person was created in the Divine Image, not in the image of another human being (Gen 1:27). If, after divorce, life needs to be reinterpreted without a spouse, it is a waste of energy to focus on hurting another human being. It saddens the spiritual within us (Eph 4:30–32). The mind will desire those wasted thoughts and questions, but it is a desire which does not help the healing process. I have heard different divorced people speak about these desires and with a grin of one-up-manship they proudly add: Yes, but revenge feels so good. True, but it does no good either.

Hate is a strong emotion that feeds on the weakness of humanity. It attempts to solve the problem of the personal embarrassment by focusing on the peccadilloes of the former spouse. Material objects are destroyed as a public witness to anger and the inner desire of one human being to obliterate another human being. If one were hurting or hating to that extent, it would be more beneficial to work on healing oneself than attacking another human being. In a simple analogy, if a person is angry about having cancer, his emotional energy (therefore his entire being) is better spent on healing and recovery of the body rather than on why he/she has cancer.

Hate and anger do not address any personal embarrassment from divorce. Hatred and anger speak loudly of the individual's pain. The destruction of property says more about the exposed wound of the individual than about an "ex" receiving a just reward. The violent actions, the divorcing of emotions in any attempt at self-rediscovery, speak of the pain of the individual, not the spouse.

Any person trying to begin life anew after having been married for a long time and attempting to address the shame of their life must focus on the reality of life. Single now, they must address life from that vantage point. They do not have nor will they have another person to put them back together. They must look at life now with their own eyes, their own opinions, their own being. Self-rediscovery is a process which looks forward rather than to the past. Self-discovery is not dependent upon the approval of an "ex" nor does it seek the answers to unanswerable questions. It recognizes the reality of divorce and understands that those questions, which beg for reasons for the divorce, are not within the human realm of a comprehensible or convincing response.

Self-discovery diminishes the embarrassment associated with divorce. Self-discovery looks to the proper healing of memories by placing them into the hands of God. Self-discovery allows the individual to see once again the Divine Image God has created in the unique self. There is no embarrassment so great that warrants the denial of moving forward in life. There is no embarrassment in human life which allows for hate and anger to consume a human being. In its greatest expression, self-discovery knits together the human dignity once again in very private ways so that a person may enter public life without any bitterness.

This is not an easy process. Like the grieving, this process of self-discovery does not occur at a specific time or in a specific space. It requires that a person move beyond personal desires of vengeance and hate. Rediscovery demands that when hateful desires emerge they be named for the evil they are. The evil in those consuming vengeful desires seeks to destroy the recovery.

How does one move beyond the self-consuming feelings of hate and anger? Even if anger or hate is justified, as in instances of familial or spousal abuse, the hatred and anger will consume the recipient of the abuse and not the abuser. This source of hatred and anger must be addressed honestly if recovery of self is to be possible. It is perfectly okay to be honest with one's feelings. They are our feelings. They do not have a value judgment. Feelings become dangerous (unhealthy) only if we allow them to consume us. Anyone consumed by anger or hatred also understands the gnawing inner desire to be healed (Jer 17:14). It is grace which the soul seeks. Only the grace of God will heal the human soul (Rom 3:24).

Healing, however, will occur only when we take the necessary steps the Lord asks from us. Jesus commands us to pray for our enemies (Matt 5:43–45). This is difficult when we are consumed by vengeful anger or even righteous anger. We are not accustomed to praying actually and less accustomed to pray for those for whom we harbor ill thoughts. The law of the Lord though remains the same. Numerous questions continually run through the mind without encountering an appropriate answer. Prayer, however, is still *the* answer.

How is it possible to pray for one who has hurt me so deeply? How is it possible for me to ask God's blessing on one who has cursed my life? How is it possible for me to seek the grace of God for one who has violated the intimacy of my heart leaving me near emotional death? How is it possible for me to pray for the one who is the cause of my pain? How is it possible for me to wish well the endeavors of the one who is the source of so much grief within me? How is it possible to pray for one who has embarrassed me to myself? How is it possible to pray for one who has shamed me before family and friends? How is it possible for me to pray for one whom I wish were dead?

These questions tear at the spiritual soul of any believer who has gone through the agony of a divorce. There is, however, a simple solution. Rooted in prayer, our feelings with all of their intense desires can be channeled into the arms of a God who truly loves us. Grieving over loss is the heart of self-rediscovery.

When we encounter those people whom we hate (the "ex", the mistress{es}, the mister{s} etc.) the Lord asks us to pray for them. There is the argument that says: I do not hate anyone not even my "ex." People lie to themselves so as not to have to address the intensity of their feelings or their hurt. It is a fallacious argument. We have great difficulty in addressing the roots of our feelings. At times, we live in an elementary mentality of our spirituality. We know that God does not want us to hate people. We know that our feelings are of anger and hate. In the contradiction of teaching and feeling, we delude ourselves by denying the feelings in some pseudo-attempt at pleasing God. God, however, knows the truth of our heart and our hurt. It would be better to address the feeling of hate and admit it to oneself and to God. Once admitted (named), the hater can seek healing.

The easiest way to address the feeling of hate is to put it honestly into the context of one's spirituality. Tell God your feeling. I hate this man. I hate this woman for whatever reason. By admitting this feeling, we acknowledge our own sinfulness before God. We understand we come before the Mercy Seat broken and unable to put into practice his Gospel. We tell the Lord we stand in need of his help in this helpless situation.

Tell God your prayer. Lord, I know you have put your Divine Image in every human being. I cannot see it in this person, and you know the reason why. Lord, I do not want to be consumed by this feeling of anger or hate; therefore, I will do what you ask of me. This simple prayer acknowledges before the ever-loving Lord that he is the eternal creator, and we are creatures. This prayer acknowledges the beauty of his Divine Image. The prayer acknowledges the role of God within our human life.

In order to learn the beautiful healing aspects of prayer begin in this manner.

1. Tell God your feeling (as suggested above).

2. Tell God your prayer (as suggested above).

3. Begin with the Lord's prayer: "Our Father . . ."

4. When you come to the end of the prayer where it states: "Deliver us from evil," replace the word "us" with the name of the person with whom you are angry.

In this very simple manner, one has begun to change the desire to obliterate into a desire of blessing. The prayer may seem stilted at the beginning because it is our tendency not to pray for those who have hurt us. Most people because of their hurt would like to ask the Lord to deliver us from the person who hurt us rather than to deliver that person from evil. Remember the intent of the prayer is: "Deliver (name) from evil."

The more this prayer is prayed, consciously asking the Lord to deliver the hated human being from evil, the more the "pray-er" becomes healed. In truth, the feelings and emotions of hate and anger associated with any divorce can consume any individual. Such despiteful feelings have ruptured our relationship with God. It is no secret what the Lord desires from us, but it is also no secret that rage and doubt have eaten at the soul. This simple prayer places the embarrassment, anger, rage, hate, abuse, and most important, the entire divorce into the hands of God. The beautiful reality of this prayer is that it is the prayer of Jesus. They are his words with our intent. This prayer, if honestly prayed, situates the confusion of divorce in the context of God's love. It is the prayer of Christian disciples for over two thousand years.

God, who knows the innermost secrets of the human heart, knows the pain of his children. God, who sent his Son into this world, knows humanity's continual need for healing. God, who desires his place within the human experience, knows how to resurrect us and breathe life into us no matter how great the loss may have been. God, who is the author of the public forum both in heaven and on earth, is the whisper in the private forum of the human heart.

CASE STUDY

The couple had been together for nearly eighteen years. They had met in post-graduate classes. They dated for some time but became serious in their relationship almost from the beginning. They were in their mid-twenties. They lived a very fast life with a lot of college partying mixed with friends and alcohol. They traveled the state for different parties as well. It was not uncommon for them to go to many different clubs in one night. They enjoyed each other immensely. Their youth propelled them to adventure together in an attempt to experience life to the fullest. Their exclusivity with each other served as a protective shield against the world for both of them. They depended upon each other for support and companionship.

Their likes and dislikes blended together as they savored every aspect of life presented to them. They particularly liked the arts: music, drama, museums, symphonies, plays, comedies, tragedies, and cultural bazaars. Their joy always found its expression in the life of the other. The couple romanced each other in the most creative of ways. They enjoyed sending provocative cards and letters to each other. They found much happiness in their flirtation.

One of the couple's interesting methods of reminding each other of their love was to sing a simple refrain from a Spanish song. There were two versions of the same line. The verse states: *En la madrugada Señor, oigo tu voz murmurando* ("In the early morning hours Lord, I hear your voice whispering"). The song itself talks about how the relationship between God and the person is a call to walk with the Lord all of one's life serving God out of love. The song stresses that God whispers the name of his servant starting each day in the early morning hours with a loving call to serve.

In public the couple could pull the other's attention away from everything else by simply humming the line. One might hum, "*En la madrugada Señor.*" The other would respond, "*Oigo tu voz murmurando.*" This simple refrain sung or hummed in public was the signal that the other party wanted to say I love you. Through this music they expressed that they depended on each other to learn about life. Through this song the couple could face anything together because they had both heard the voice of God in the early morning hours. *En la madrugada Señor* was their simple secret code of love, but it referred to a love based on growing up together with God in their marriage.

The importance and significance of this song cannot be downplayed because one of the parties did not speak Spanish. To be able to sing the refrain meant that this one had gone beyond the United States's cultural tendency and deficiency of mono-lingualism. It meant this person understood the beauty of reaching into another culture to experience a greater reality of life. Rare are the moments when in an intercultural relationship does one party go beyond the dominant language and culture (usually English) to enter into the Latino cultural reality of language, music, food, traditions, and life vision. It takes great effort for one to attempt another language and risk the mistakes in pronunciation, declensions, and meaning. The singing or humming of the refrain, therefore, showed the deep involvement and commitment of the relationship.

They were never shy about showing their affection. At times, they even expressed that affection in inappropriate places. They had no qualms about expressing their private affection in the most public of places. They knew better, but loved the idea that people could engage in a bit of voyeurism. The couple found it even more appealing that the voyeurism was directed towards them. They wanted the world to know they were in love with each other.

The young woman indulged in an incident of infidelity during the dating period. The young man was devastated. Within two months, he asked his fiancée to marry him. He was devastated by the infidelity but suppressed his feelings. The fiancée confessed the infidelity one night as the couple lay in bed. The tears began and the young man left the bed and went to sleep in the living room. He could not understand the infidelity. Supposedly forgiving the fiancée, he asked for her hand in marriage. The young man never forgave his spouse; he didn't know how. Anger and rage at the infidelity were buried deep within his psyche. At that time he told himself through a vow that he would never let another human being hurt him in such a manner ever again. The anger and rage would surface later in his own infidelities during the married years.

During those eighteen years, this couple grew up together. In their entertainment activities, they played together wholeheartedly. Above all else, they enjoyed their recreation with each other. In moments of play, they encountered once again the joyful moments of their dating period. Those times of play allowed both to discover again the person with whom they had fallen in love. Their romancing and public flirting with each other went well beyond that of most couples. Their lives began to blend: they knew each other's stories and jokes; they knew each other's thought patterns; and they had spent so many years together that they also began to take each other for granted. Still, it was not uncommon in a mall or in a car ride to hear one sing *"en la madrugada Señor"* with a response quickly begun on the last note.

The husband could not imagine life without his spouse. He saw their marriage as one entity. The wife, however, began to go out with other friends. At first, it was nothing, but then it began to take on greater dimensions. The wife spent more time playing with friends. With little time with her husband, she found more time for infidelities.

Both spouses had jobs which allowed them to have the week after Christmas off from work. The husband always took the week off while the wife always decided to work all or part of that week. The husband would plead with her to take the time off so that they could spend time together for a real vacation. Their jobs had taken too much of their playtime away from them so the husband sought honestly more time after Christmas. The wife, however, would not relent and continued to work the week after Christmas. The year before the breakup of the marriage she worked the week after Christmas instead of taking time off with her husband. The job, however, required the wife to go as a representative of the company on a ski trip with high school youth.

The husband was furious. It was the ultimate insult. Without being required to go, she had opted for the ski trip, sacrificing the couple's private recreational time for a public outing. For the husband, it was the clear indication that things were very wrong in the relationship. He felt within his heart that he had been cheated on again. The spouse had chosen to play without him. This action hurt the husband in unspeakable ways, and the spouse never had a clue (or at least never admitted to the knowledge) about the hidden message of this action. The spouse continued to harbor the fantasy that the ski trip was part of her job; therefore, nothing had been sacrificed from the marriage. Participating in this outing did not shake the spouse at all, despite her husband's anger and disappointment.

This incident was the tip of an iceberg, masking the deeper problems in the marriage. It stands out like a dangerous dalliance that the couple was experiencing deeper problems in their communication with each other. It highlights problems in their recreational moments together. Those times, which were used to rediscover each other, now posed a problem. The desire not to vacation with a spouse is to say through one's actions: I do not want this relationship to be re-created in wholeness; I do not desire the examination it requires, nor am I willing to exert the energy it may demand from me; I do not want to play with you.

Within a year the couple divorced. Looking back in reflection, the recreational moments speak the loudest of the joys and the troubles within the relationship. Those recreational moments, the vacations and the outings, became the times where the couple played out their unspoken feelings. As the relationship soured, vacations and adventures became the focal point of intense feelings, both positive and negative.

Fewer times together ceased to be recreational. They were now moments of two individuals sightseeing together. Fun was not found in the other. The husband found his pleasure instead in numerous affairs hidden from his spouse. The spouse found pleasure in the outings with friends, both male and female. The night clubbing, drinking, and partying with non-mutual friends proved more desirable and recreational for her than going anywhere with the husband. She sought the divorce from the husband. In the aftermath, the husband called her trying to learn what had occurred.

I am so ignorant. It took me a couple of days to put things together. I called and asked if there was someone else in the picture. Something had to explain the cause of the divorce. It took me some time before I figured it out. There must have been someone else taking my place. I asked if she were having an affair. I knew that I had been unfaithful. My spouse replied.

I don't think that is the issue.

After eighteen years of marriage I think I have the right to ask anything I want, don't you?

Yes I have been with someone else.

Who?

You don't know him . . . there have been several different people. I just need more companionship than you can give me. I thought that we could possibly remain friends, but I realize that this too will be impossible.

You don't even want to be friends?

No! I do not think we can maintain a friendship. It will be too difficult. I don't want to be friends. You do not even know how to be a friend! The best thing for both of us is to end this completely with no contact.

A year later the husband still had strong feelings for his ex-spouse. One night alone he drank to excess. His drunken behavior took him into frightening memories as he began to look upon the loneliness of his life. His friends and family had told him to get on with life. The ex-spouse was not worth his health, but the husband still had his bouts with tears and memories. Those tears and memories became heightened by the self-medicating alcohol remedy he sought to ease his pain. He still wanted some type of relationship with his "ex", but it was not going to happen. His excessive drinking resurrected painful memories of friendship and rejection:

I knew I was drinking too much. I got on my knees and cried to God. I screamed asking questions to no one there. With tears in my eyes, I saw myself going down into a tear-filled nothing. I told myself that I was having a nervous breakdown. I was afraid that if I had a breakdown, I would lose my mind completely. I screamed crying for someone to catch me so that I would not fall. I was on my knees, yet I knew that I was going to hit bottom. I was so scared. I opened my mouth but could say nothing, and then, I saw the most horrible thing in my mind. I saw my own face screaming back at me. My eyes were full of tears. It was like looking into a mirror. In my mind, I cried until I finally hugged myself. It was the most terrifying moment of my memories. In the background the music played *en la madrugada Señor*, and I realized that now I learned I was all alone. I miss the friend of my life. At times I want to call and check in. I am better now, but I miss the friendship greatly. Eighteen years is a long time. We grew up together. With my spouse, I learned everything about life. When I see a full moon now, I know there is a wonderful light on the other side. I wonder if my "ex" sees the same moon and ever thinks of me? I wonder if my "ex" hears the whispers of God *en la madrugada* still?

PASTORAL REFLECTION

For centuries we have grown so accustomed to the grandiose and majestic titles of the Lord Jesus. We, in our desire to show him how much we love and respect him, have attributed to him words and titles beyond ordinary speech: consubstantial, transcendent, omnipresent, omniscient, Pantocrator, co-equal and co-eternal with the Trinity. The titles speak more of our reverence than of our relationship: Sacred Heart, King of Kings, Lord of Lords, Prince of Peace, Divine Love. Words and titles demonstrate to the world of believers and non-believers that we hold our greatest respect for Jesus. He is God. One of the consequences of the myriad of devotional titles and references is that they tend to remove us more and more from the very personal relationship Jesus wants with us.

The Scripture reminds us that our starting point, as a people of faith, is that God has loved us from the beginning (1 John 4:10). Every other aspect of our life is a testament to being loved by God. God does not remove himself through our titles or words. No matter how he is addressed or worshipped, his desire remains the same: to live and dwell within the human heart (Acts 17:28).

One of the most consistent titles in the Gospels used for Jesus is the one which our culture seems to have replaced for the more devotional and majestic titles. It is the title of Teacher. Although the Scriptures are replete with the image of Jesus as the Teacher with his own disciples, I think that somehow we have relegated him to the position of God, at times so inaccessible that we are not willing to listen as student disciples. At times, it is easier for people to relate to the divinity of Jesus and miss the beauty of his humanity. The Scriptures, however, love to refer to him as Teacher (John 20:16). It shows us how the early Christian communities viewed him as part of their daily lives. He was, above all else, the One who loved them enough to teach them.

Although there are many places where Scripture presents Jesus as the Teacher, there are two which offer themselves as ideal in reflecting the image of the compassionate educator. The first is the passage of the beatitudes found in the Gospel of Matthew, chapter 5. This is the beginning of the wonderful Sermon on the Mount. In all of the richness found in Jesus' sermon, it is the action that precedes the words that demonstrate clearly the role Jesus sought and seeks.

The chapter begins by saying that when he saw the crowds of people, Jesus went up to the mountain. The disciples gather around him. Jesus begins to speak and teach them. This simple action is repeated in prayer many times over with the disciples of the present day. The Lord sees us desiring us to gather around him so that he might speak and teach. I imagine this scene with great awe.

Imagine the people from every walk of life. They are opposites in every imaginable way: wealthy and poor, smelling bad or good; full of sin in their lives; adulterers and liars; thieves or blasphemers; they covet beyond measure. They have at times worshipped other gods. They are abusers of every sort: spousal, familial, substances, physical, emotional, and psychological.

Among them are prayerful parents desiring the best for their children and at the same time giving the worst example of parenthood. Some are doubters and believers, merchants and tax collectors. Some are people who survive by forming their own lives, their own ideas of right and wrong. Some are the homeless coming for free food or any handout available. They have God at a convenient location within their heart so as to be able to tap into him when they need him. Like most of us, they want God in their life when it is convenient for them.

They are alcoholics, heterosexual and homosexual, fornicators, or married people in lustful violation of their vows. They are the healthy and the sick. They are divorced people. They are young people grabbing life with a vision of how they will run things. They are old people bemoaning the past and wondering why they are still alive. They are self-righteous people full of secret sins they will reveal to no one. They are the most prayerful and apparently grace-filled people. They are the most sinful people. They are people who follow all 613 laws of the Old Testament. They are people who mock even the existence of God. There is little difference between the listeners of yesterday and today. This was the crowd who came to listen at the feet of the Teacher; they are the sea of humanity.

Then the most beautiful thing happens. The Word of God spoke, just like in the beginning, and from the chaos of life, Jesus teaches them. The words that follow, the beatitudes, are prayerful and consoling words found now in the Scripture and probably often repeated in Jesus' life. Their intent, however, is a much deeper reality for all of us. Jesus, looking upon this sea of humanity, in all of its brokenness (sin), saw the Divine

Image and reminded them that no matter the situation in which they found themselves, they were blessed.

He reminded them in his teaching that God has loved them from the very beginning, and he has not withdrawn his blessing. He spoke to the chaotic aspects of their life (mourning, the desire for righteousness and humility, for justice, peace and wholeness) and told them they had found God's blessing. God, despite the chaos of human living, had never abandoned them.

Jesus reminded them that the Kingdom of Heaven was not found in the future, but that it was a present reality when one recognized ultimate dependency (poverty of spirit) on God for everything. He taught them that blessing was born out of a relationship with the Almighty. He taught them that blessing was even found and glorified when persecution resulted from love for God. He taught them that God loved them. If they recognized only this point, then everything else would fall into a grace-filled order.

There is another beautiful story which illustrates Jesus as the Teacher. It is found in the Gospel of John, chapter 20. It is the story of Mary Magdalene wandering around the cemetery looking for the body of the one whom she loves. She enters into banter with the resurrected Jesus mistaking him for a gardener. The scene is filled with the most tender of moments recorded by the early Christian believers.

She is weeping in a cemetery and is still probed as to why she cries. She is at the stage of grief, lost in her thoughts and memories, recalling the moments of her life, her anger and joy. Like anyone in a cemetery, she is crying for the one she loves. Her mind is lost in the "ifs" of life: If she could only say one last thing to him; if she could only see him one last time; if she could only let him know how much he meant to her; if she could only embrace him, then she would be consoled.

Then the most beautiful thing happens. The Word of God spoke her name, just like in the beginning of their personal relationship, and from the chaos of grief and death, Jesus taught her again. The scripture records her response as "Rabboni." The scholars and translators teach us that this speaks of a personal relationship. The Spanish text translates the word as "my teacher." Regardless of how it is articulated, a new relationship with the Risen Christ has begun.

The Lord has determined the structure of this relationship. He will call his disciple by his/her name. The disciple, like a sheep, will hear the voice of the shepherd and will respond. In the hearing of one's name being called by God, life takes on a new purpose. The relationship between God and humankind is not based on edicts and commands but rooted in the gentle whisper of personal identity (1 Kgs 19:11–13a). It is a teacher-student relationship once again. God's voice desires to teach a student so that the student can transform the world. The response is so personal that the student understands how much this teacher is willing to do for him. He is not just Teacher; he is My Teacher.

It is clear that every Gospel presents Jesus as Teacher. The living Word still seeks the hearts of his disciples, us, so that we might be willing like Mary, Martha's sister, or the Magdalene to sit at his feet, listen, and learn (Luke 10:38–42). Jesus is still the Teacher to those who desire to follow him. It is our life that he desires to transform. It is our manner of thinking and acting that he seeks to illumine, so that his vision might be ours and not vice-versa. He says that where he is will be the place where his disciple is (John 17:24).

He will be the Teacher, and we shall be the students. The classes are a little larger since Gospel times, but the text and class material are the same. We must take what he has taught us and appropriate it to our own life experiences. Both stories, the beatitudes and the Magdalene, remind us of our potential relationship with the risen Lord Jesus which resonates at the very core of our human heart. He is the Teacher who has used his life, death, and resurrection to instruct us in every detail of our life, long or short. With the risen Lord, in love we have learned that a week has more than seven days, and we celebrate our eighth day with him. Nothing is impossible for God.

The couple was so enamored with each other that they found a song which could take them back to happier moments of their life. They used one refrain to describe their relationship. They knew in the deepest parts of their heart that each one had taught the other very important lessons of life. Above all else, they learned how to play together, to recreate with each other. With a simple song refrain, they could even capture the other's attention no matter where they found themselves. They could hear the whispering voice of God. Their friendship, however, lost sight of the larger picture of their life together with one another and with God.

The focusing of life into only the recreational moments or placing such heavy emphasis on those moments to share feelings and communication consumed the couple's relationship until it could not breathe. The recreational time had become a time to resolve issues instead of a time for rediscovery of the other person. The suffocation was unbearable because all the feelings and emotions had been centered into too few moments, which supposedly had been meant for play.

The sadness in this relationship is the loss of friendship. They did learn together about life. In their play, they did teach other about emotions and feelings. Being together for so long did entail a growing experience so entwined that divorce would mean having to learn about life and love from a whole new angle, as a single person. The difficulty in this relationship was that at different periods of their life together, one was the teacher and the other the student. As they interchanged these roles protecting themselves from outside influences, it became confusing to try to distinguish who was teacher and who was student.

Although each one could hum the refrain at any given point, learning does not imply permanence. To be able to hear the "whispering voice of God in the early morning hours" does not mean that one wants to stay forever in a relationship which does not offer companionship. Learning, however, did take place.

Memories cannot be erased from either partner. There will always be references to that other human being with whom they shared life. A song on the radio, a museum visit, a play, a Mexican fiesta, and other significant symbolic acts will take hold of either party at any given time and remind them that they experienced life (and learned about it) with someone they loved. Whoever is touched will know life by what has been experienced from the previous lover.

Even though divorce has occurred, life still holds those memories, the good and the bad, tight within the memory box. No matter what occurs in the future, the past private events play themselves out like a tragedy in the forum of the human psyche. Even if subsequent relationships occur, this divorced couple will use the relationship from which they learned about life to compare, judge, and change all subsequent relationships. They grew up together. Divorce does not terminate or eliminate what they taught each other.

Jesus is still the Teacher of his disciples. We have grown up with him. He still gathers us around himself to pronounce blessings upon us. He still calls us by our own name that we might see his risen presence and move beyond the chaos of our life. He still whispers in the early morning hours. At every moment of our life, we have learned what he desires from us. He has been in our work, our homes, and our families. He has even been in our recreation. Stop and think of all the things he has taught us about life and love. Stop and think of all the things he still desires to teach. Imagine the chaos life would be if we had no knowledge of the consummate Teacher. Imagine the chaos life would be for us if we thought we had all of the answers. Recall the chaos life is when we take over the role of Teacher.

Divorce is no exception when it comes to the desires of the Teacher to teach. Jesus, if we truly acknowledge him as Lord, still holds the answers to healing the broken hearted, to giving life to the lifeless. Divorce attacks with a demolishing force breaking everything in its path, even friendships. Couples do enjoy each other at times, but the reality of divorce is strong enough to block any memory of the good times. Divorce thrashes the relationship and eventually convinces the participants that their marriage was a farce even before it began.

Jesus is not absent from the divorce. Jesus is not absent from the relationship. He heard every argument and lived through every word of anger. He even wept at the times of hate, and in the early morning hours he even whispered names once again. He does not absent himself at the first hint of problems. He does not excuse himself when the tension in the room thickens.

On the contrary, the Lord has been with this couple from its beginning. He too desired that this marriage would be a blessing to the world. He too desired that this marriage would be the showpiece of love and forgiveness. He entered into this relationship with the desire that all three would work together for better and worse.

Understandably, Jesus holds a dual position. He desired to be the couple's first love in their human relationship. If they had listened, he would have taught them that his presence was in each of them. If they had paid attention, they would have seen his blessings in every moment. If they had listened closely, they would have heard his voice teaching them about marriage and its principles of success: mutuality, communication, sexuality, mutual spirituality, play, loving the other before oneself, trust, fidelity, forgiveness, love which seeks the good of the other and works to provide that good.

Divorce illustrates the couple's failure to listen to the Teacher, but it does not imply that the Teacher is absent. The Teacher still teaches. Even when the divorce is final, and hate has had its day, the Teacher comes to teach how to rebuild one's life apart from hate. He still provides the means of loving oneself so as to be able to move into the grace of healing. The Sermon on the Mount still calls the disciples to recognize that their lives, with the joys and pains, are blessed. His call to faith still teaches that God is calling his people to peace out of the chaos of divorce from which they have come.

For centuries Christ's students have gathered to hear his voice. For centuries his disciples have come to be fed through his Scripture. For centuries his chosen daughters and sons have opened their hearts putting them at the disposal of the Teacher. We have learned from him that forgiveness is the answer. He has taught us to pray for those whom we hate. He has taught us that we are blessed from the beginning. He continues to teach the beauty of the Divine Image within each of us. He teaches us the dignity of all human life even within the one who has been the cause of our grief or pain. With Jesus, we have heard his whispers *en la madrugada*.

PRAYER FOR UNDERSTANDING

Lord Jesus, you are my teacher.
You teach me the language of love,
how to write with forgiveness,
how to stay in the lines
of human respect and dignity.

Lord Jesus, you are my teacher.
You provide the recess
from work and fatigue.
You provide the food
of eternal life.
You teach me
how to share.

Lord Jesus you are my teacher
of right and wrong,
of sin and grace
of peace and wholeness.
Because of you
I repent.

5

Take Care of Yourself

IVORCE IS NEVER FINAL. Divorce is a public action which terminates a marriage, but the reality of the divorce and its consequences affect the future lives of ex-husbands and wives. Some never quite recover. The feelings and emotions are strong enough to carry over into the life of each individual for many years and surface at unexpected moments years later. Time may pass, but the harshness of having shared a life with someone else and the tragedy of having seen that life shattered is powerfully imprinted on the soul. Divorce is a wound one will carry throughout life. Divorce recalls the confusion which recurs in memory, counseling, or reflection.

There are stages in the emotional process of divorce which need to be recognized and addressed. Although there are many variations especially when children are involved, the stages can be categorized into four: Reaction, Truth, Encounter, and Future. These stages provide the overall basis of working out the consequences of divorce in life.

Each stage is rife with its own dangers and pitfalls for the divorced. Each stage has its own proper length and is not limited to any definite amount of time. Stages may overlap into each other allowing the person to experience many different emotions simultaneously. Depending on whether one is the initiator or the recipient of the divorce, each stage holds different consequences for both parties.

REACTION

"It's all I've thought about for two weeks"

For all of the inconsistencies of life, divorce is rarely a surprise. When a party in the marriage views the divorce as a surprise, it indicates a lack of honest communication between the married partners. Both individuals are aware of past problems which have somehow been consciously or unconsciously ignored. Both have used the same excuse: "That's just the way I am; if you don't like it, then there's the door." Both have been frustrated by the lack of change in the other's life. Both parties have not made any changes in their own personal lives. Divorce does not come as a surprise, but it does come as a nearly deadly blow to all involved.

From both parties, divorce provokes very strong feelings about everything in the marriage. It reaches into the past and drags out every piece of dirty linen, real or imagined. Divorce airs every argument a husband or wife can remember. It narrows any fruitful discussion into the smallest of details demanding an understandable answer as to why something occurred in the past. The parties actually believe that if they receive the unanswerable answer that they will understand what went wrong in the marriage or, at the least, who was primarily responsible for the break up.

Divorce pitches each one against the other as it futilely attempts to make sense of the chaos. Divorce does not try to fix the marriage. It makes no attempt to make things right between the couple. Divorce declares the end of marriage. The consequences are devastating.

The confrontational period, when the divorce is announced, begins the REACTION stage. Of all the stages, this is the most traumatic. This is the break. This is the moment when everything comes crashing in on the integrity of the whole family; children and relatives on both sides complicate the situation. This is the moment when the farce of a good marriage is unmasked, and the entire world is exposed to the hate-filled life of two very broken people. This is the time when each one has to face the horrible reality that love is now lost. They see each other in total nakedness and do not want to be together. It is the moment when their vows or commitment lack fortitude. Both have little memory of wedding, infatuation, or ephemeral happiness. The vows make no sense to them.

In the REACTION stage, the memory of the vows become personal rather than shared. In their reflection, a couple will remember how he/she lived the vows for better or worse. They will recall their own fidelity to the holy promises and see very clearly where the other one has not kept faith. Each one takes shelter in his/her own sanctity as they point out the sins of this broken relationship.

When the break is made by announcement or papers served, an incredible sadness occurs. The grief is as powerful as the grief of death. A marriage has died. Hate follows. The recipient of the news hates the divorcing spouse. The initiator of the divorce hates the mess of having to face the reality of pain inflicted.

The recipient hates beyond measure. With the intensity of pain, it is not uncommon for the recipient even to wish the death of the divorcing spouse. The emotions are extreme, even wishing every type of evil upon the one once wished every blessing. The hurt knows no bounds.

The feelings, in this REACTION stage, surface daily as the reality of divorce settles in. Although feelings may dissipate or ameliorate in the future, they never wholly disappear. Feelings of loss, hate, and failure return at indiscriminate times to remind the recipient of the brokenness. These feelings return without warning and find expression in the lyrics of a song, a scene in a movie, a memory associated with an object, a piece of clothing, a wedding ring, a love scene in a restaurant, a simple dressing in the morning, watching an old video, or a cry in the shower.

Over time, feelings linger in memory, rising unbidden at the weakest moment of a person's life, to prey on the human psyche. As a person begins to heal from divorce, the memory will still try to remind the person of personal failure at life together.

The initiator too suffers the feelings of loss, hate, and failure. He too must address his life from the viewpoint of a mistake in relationship. He too will be reminded by objects and memories of the painful relationship that existed because of lack of honesty. Many couples who divorce want the entire thing to be completed and will state: "I don't want anything; I just want out." This attempt at erasing the memory by eliminating every material object that reminds them of the spouse is futile.

At any given time, the memory will poke at the mind of the initiator and remind him of the time he spent with someone he said he loved. He too must ask himself what is the error in his life which did not allow love to grow as both changed. Memories are located in the mind not in a picture or card.

The initiator too must address the reasons for the divorce. As divorce becomes a reality in his life, he too must ask why he was in the relationship in the first place. He must address the issue of his own culpability in the failure of the marriage. His living experience, now that he is divorced, may tell him he is free, but his memory will always remind him of a previous tie. It cannot be forgotten. The memory of that relationship will always cry for forgiveness.

The REACTION stage is the most painful. It begins the barrage of hate toward the other. The REACTION stage is where the situation demands termination as quickly as possible. There are many tears during this stage. It hurts. This stage is filled with the struggle to sort out the memories. This time is dedicated to trying to find out what went wrong. This time poses the options of reconciliation (if possible) or retaliation or acceptance. With the confusion of feelings in the REACTION stage, all three options are debated, argued, and considered. These three options are taken to the extremes as the couple tries to make sense out of a painful hurt.

In the extremes, the options can become violent. As months pass, these options do not disappear. In conjunction with the feelings and memories, they too present themselves to the individuals with all the same doubts and questions. There is no easy solution. The solution is lived one day at a time in an attempt to put the pieces of life back together for two broken human beings.

One couple had to face the reality of their broken relationship. The husband came home and lay on the bed exhausted from work. His desire for his spouse prompted him to be ready for sexual play. The spouse came in and found the husband lying nude on the bed desiring the afternoon for them. The spouse said that they needed to talk. Perhaps it would be better to talk somewhere else like at the beach. The husband said that he was tired of talking. He just wanted to lie down and have sex. The spouse withdrew insisting that they needed to talk.

The spouse stated that sex was not even an option anymore. They really needed to talk. The husband realized that the situation was graver than what he expected.

You don't want to have sex with me?

No.

You don't want to be with me?

No.

What are you saying? You don't want to be married anymore?

The spouse nodded in agreement.

You want to be un-married?

The nod continued.

You want a divorce?

The nod said yes.

The tears began. There was no yelling or screaming. The husband lay on the bed and told his spouse with tears coming from his eyes (or heart), "I am going to miss you." Then, he realized he was naked and felt great shame. He quickly put on his clothes and drove to his parents' house. He was a grown man going to his parents' home who lived quite a distance away. The shame grew within him until he was completely engulfed in his own embarrassment. He was inundated with questions and doubts, memories and tears. It was raining as he drove home. His mind was not on the road. With his mind on other concerns and not the driving, the husband almost crashed into semi-trucks in other lanes. He stopped to phone his spouse.

I can't deal with this. I don't know how. Is this really what you want?

It's all I've thought about for two weeks.

As divorce became reality, the husband's love and acceptance moved into rage and anger. Hate began in words he uttered to himself as he began to build his life. He realized some of the selfishness of his spouse. The spouse could not even mention the word "divorce." It was the husband who had to decipher the nods. It was he who had to say the word "divorce" because his spouse could not even address the issue honestly. Then in the epitome of not caring, it was the spouse who let the husband drive off in blinding rain with so many things on his mind. The husband would recall the incident later.

Two weeks, 14 days, what about my life? What about the years of our marriage? What about my feelings? I hate my "ex."

The REACTION stage had begun.

TRUTH

"Hey, do you know. . . ?"

The second stage, TRUTH, is a consequence of the reaction stage. As the reaction stage wanes, the divorced person can't help wondering about the life of the "ex." In the initial months of the divorce, as any of the options of reconciliation, revenge, or acceptance fail to be realized, a divorcing person will naturally wonder about the "ex." It is not always a healthy speculation. Sometimes the wondering is to make one feel better by contrast. If there is anger, the wonderment is geared toward revenge and hoping the other is suffering. Sometimes the wondering is done to prove to oneself that he or she is healed or healing. It is done to show that life can go on without any help from any "ex."

This wondering is natural to the initiator and the recipient. It can evoke powerful feelings of resentment or spite. It pulls from memories to speculation on how life is being lived in the absence of a spouse. The past will always pose potential problems as it is now viewed with a different lens—the lens of loss.

The holidays are the most difficult of times for wondering. Holidays, birthdays, and anniversaries evoke great and painful memories that bring no joy (or less joy than regrets for missed opportunities). Thanksgiving and Christmas take their toll on the human mind as one looks back at life, love, and mistakes. The holidays pose the danger of depression because they are family times. They hold the ideals of idyllic relationship. They remind us of what is good about life. They speak to us of peace, laughter, holy moments, and moments of grace. Holidays remind us of deep friendships that have forged our lives. They remind us that in the eyes of God, we are worth everything.

Depression occurs because of the tension within ourselves in accepting the goodness God has placed there and denying the overpowering messages of the world, that tries to re-create us in its image. This is a constant human struggle. God has told us that we are worth his Son. The world tells us that our worth is determined by the way we look, act, smell, and think. The holidays become depressing at times because they highlight and magnify the tension in which we live. In divorce situations, the values of the world hold an ace in their hand reminding the divorced that another human being has determined he or she is worth nothing. This is a lie but a wounding arrow nonetheless. The divorced person need only look within his life to see that Christ is the trump card.

It is not uncommon, therefore, for divorced people to experience a depression during the holiday period. There is so much reflection on the family and God that their personal failure may seem magnified or exaggerated. It is not uncommon for them also to wonder about their "ex." They think of past holidays, the good ones and the terrifying. They recall the extended families and question their boundaries now with former in-laws. Are they divorced from them too? Have those relationships changed as well? When you divorce do you divorce the whole extended family too? Do you send a Christmas card?

These may seem like silly questions, but they involve a wide range of feelings and emotions. They demand answers that are highly unique to the individual. They pose situations that neither party thought about when the divorce was sought. They provide moments that illustrate that divorce has complicated life for many people not just two.

Divorce terminates a marriage, but it does not terminate thoughts or feelings. Wondering about the spouse for any reason whatsoever or whenever, not just on holidays, points to the fact this marriage and pending divorce has long-lasting consequences. It takes its toll for many years.

Families and friends provide little help in the wondering moments. They are quick to repeat the gossip and make innuendoes to ex-spouses about the other one. They are quick to mention who is going out with whom or where they recently saw an "ex." They are not shy about mentioning these facts in front of other family members or in a public forum. They are not concerned about sharing this information (gossip) with any friends who will listen. They are careless about bad mouthing the "ex" and exaggerating his faults. They are quick to answer questions about whereabouts and activities. They know more about the life of the "ex" than does the previous spouse.

Gossip (which is still a sin) and rumors abound. More often than not, after the divorce, the life of the "ex" is shown for what it is by families and friends. This is a time when the faults and sins of the "ex" are talked about openly. They tell of infidelities and irresponsibility. Divorce gives everyone permission to open the book of life and read the pages of marital abuse, alcoholism, rigidity, sexual deviance, or immorality.

The TRUTH stage thrives on the wondering. It is almost masochistic. In many ways wondering about the life of an "ex" is a self-punishing attitude attempting to heal one's wounds. The TRUTH stage allows for the wondering to take center stage in the mind and cause appropriate confusion. The TRUTH stage looks to the gossip and rumor to feed the wonder and ease the hunger for knowledge about the other. Pain, however, does not go away with knowledge. It continues to hurt as different people explain their own relationship with an "ex."

Two women worked for a company in different branch locations in different areas of the state. They were both presenters at a company workshop. One came into the room for her presentation as the other one was closing down. They began to talk about the company and their jobs. They didn't know each other but knew people in common.

One lady realized that the other woman worked in the department of a friend of hers. As they realized their common knowledge about an acquaintance, they began to laugh. The second woman began to inquire more.

If you know that guy then . . . Hey, do you know . . . ?

She mentioned the name of the first woman's husband. They had only been divorced for two months.

Yes, I do know him. He's wild . . . he is one crazy person

How do you know him?

All three of us go out every now and then . . .There's nothing he won't do.

She gave the first woman a smile and wink never knowing this woman was the previous wife. The first woman conducted her workshop, went into her hotel room, and cried. This was the woman with whom her husband had had an extra-marital affair. This was the lady who had taken her sexual place. This was the woman whom her husband told her that she didn't know. This was the woman ("the bitch, the slut, the whore") whom her husband thrived on for sex. This was the lie she had been living with for the last seven months or more. She wondered how many other women there were. She cried and cursed the woman, the women, the friend, and her husband.

She realized, when she calmed down, she was divorced. The pain overwhelmed her. She was an educated professional woman devastated by the penis mentality of a shallow human being, her ex-husband. She hated him. She hated his promiscuity. Her wonder now turned to rage as she cursed his life for all that he had put her through in this divorce and for all that he was still putting her through in this post-divorce. She screamed to God to damn his soul, to thwart his projects, to un-create him. In a brief instant of rationality, she realized the implications of her meeting with the other woman. All her memories are now tainted. Her holidays and her wondering begin with a curse. She knows better, but she is bitter.

Tell me who she is.

You don't know them.

There's a bunch?

It's not that important. That's not what this divorce is about.

The divorce caused her to wonder even more about her past. She wondered about the future. How many more times does she have to face her humiliation so blatantly?

I hate my "ex."

The TRUTH stage had begun.

ENCOUNTER

"Can't you see I still love you?"

The third stage, ENCOUNTER, forces the couple to face the reality of divorce after physical separation occurs. Divorce demands physical separation. The REACTION stage allows for the struggling feelings and emotions as they surface in an attempt to put life together. The REACTION stage is painful because physical separation has taken place. It is a separation and termination mandated by a civil magistrate. Life has begun without the other person. The sorting out of feelings and emotions is time consuming and exhausting. The REACTION stage causes confusion as it tries to bring a sense of order to life.

The TRUTH stage allows the person to make sense of a larger picture. As painful as it may be to face the truth of the past, the TRUTH stage allows the person to put truth into the broader scenario. Truth of the past marriage surfaces. The aftermath of divorce and its consequences with all the hidden moments of pain exposed for all to face can be a healing stage if used correctly—to move beyond pain into living. The TRUTH stage allows for the divorced person to face the truth, to face oneself honestly. Encountering the former lover face to face, however, is a greater show than any soap opera could possibly hope to provide.

The ENCOUNTER stage, if it is to be approached healthily, requires that the participants know and love themselves. This is not easy because the self-restraint, which is required, must incorporate the feelings and emotions of a difficult past with the integrity and honesty of life as it is currently being lived. The ENCOUNTER stage requires an honesty that admits that both individuals hold culpability in the disintegration of the marriage. It requires that neither one blame the other for anything. It requires a respect that life has continued, moved on without the presence of the ex-spouse.

The ENCOUNTER stage demands that the individuals face each other after a period of separation has occurred. It is never an easy encounter. Too many mental arguments have occurred. Each person has argued, cried, and debated every issue in the absence of the other. Because of the lapse of time, very serious monologues have occurred as each person has tried to make sense of life after the divorce. Even though these monologues are filled with painful emotions and feelings, they contain serious matter about the marriage/divorce. The fact that this matter was never discussed constructively during the marriage period exposes the travesty.

Other mistakes have been made since the divorce. The rebound effect has already occurred. Each person has ignored his own vulnerability, her own fragility. They have licked their wounds with the salve of self-pity and self-justification. Each one has entered into questionable friendships and relationships trying to ease the pain of divorce. Each one justified him-herself to satisfaction. Each one has sorted out the divorce mentally by rationalizing the events and convicting the previous lover thus shifting culpability in the other direction.

The ENCOUNTER stage brings out again the many emotions which have surfaced since the physical separation. The ENCOUNTER stage, therefore comes armed with the different emotions and situations which have occurred since the moment of marital termination. That rush of emotions has to be sorted out so that the first encounter is not dominated by any one emotion. The ENCOUNTER stage brings moments when the previous spouses have to face each other.

This is a painful moment of reality for both of them. Each one wrestles with the emotional memories that have plagued the mind since the separation. It is useless to argue (though it happens) because they are arguing about things that do not matter. The mere appearance of the other individual has the potential to evoke hate-filled thoughts of revenge, an anger so intense it may express itself in violence. Emotionally, seeing the other person provokes thoughts of ill will, even death. Divorce has caused so much hurt that the initial meeting with the previous spouse is one of trepidation, at worst, and uneasiness, at best. The last time they met painful things had been said to each other. Hurtful words and painful memories were their last experience together.

The last meeting of the spouses was not a healthy experience. It was the shattering of their illusion of marriage. It was the moment when love became hate. It was the moment when the lie of their relationship gave way to the truth. It was a time of tears, shouting, accusations, and wounding each other. It was a time of blaming.

Now as one faces the other, each is situated in opposing chairs with equal ammunition at their fingertips. Emotionally, they are on an even playing field. When the divorce was announced the grieving time was extended. Now both spouses have had time to grieve personally. Time has given each one the ability to rebuild life from different resources. The initial meeting is a new battleground for the previous spouses. It evokes different feelings and emotions. It demands self-restraint and the grace to move beyond oneself if the encounter is to be civil.

The ENCOUNTER stage is a delicate time. Civility should be the goal. The reality of one's emotions and feelings toward all of the pain which has been experienced stands as a natural contradiction to any desired civility. This encounter places the participants in the public arena of human life while asking them to be civil to each other knowing very well that enemies are rarely civil. This social encounter risks the embarrassment of exposing the lesion of divorce as the festering wound it really is.

The ENCOUNTER stage sets the theater for the public to witness the impact the divorce has taken on each individual. The stage is ready for the public to see the hidden pain of the individuals. As public as the marriage was, this encounter is an even bigger undertaking. It is an encounter everyone awaits and no none relishes.

Regardless of understanding what this stage requires, it is usually experienced with feelings of disgust for the other individual. There is a natural tendency to engage in one last argument, one last game of winning (one last blaming). The feelings can be so strong that they negate any civility whatsoever and return to the fighting which mirrors the causes of the divorce. The ENCOUNTER stage reminds the participants that divorce is never final. It is also a foreshadowing that future encounters will have to occur whether one likes it or not. This first encounter is the manifestation that life does continue. The participants are the framers of whether the future will be lived positively or negatively. It is the preview of the future meetings which will take place.

The couple had an amicable divorce promising to keep in touch with each other. One spouse did not want the divorce but knew it was futile to try and keep someone in a relationship when the other one wanted out of it. It still did not remove any of the pain of divorce nor did it reduce the emotional trauma associated with divorce. It was a simple letting go of the relationship with each other. They knew that their lives had been intrinsically intertwined with each other. Why fight about things? Their arguing had been reduced drastically. As they let go they made queer promises to each other that they would inform each other about the health of the families because of a general concern for the in-laws.

There was no contact with each other for five months since the divorce. One night there was a message that a grandmother had died. The time of the funeral arrangements and burial were left on the answering machine. The ex-spouses lived in different cities. The attendance at the funeral would take at least five hours by car. The decision to attend the funeral was one made out of respect for the deceased but also with the hidden desire to see the ex-spouse. The drive to the funeral brought back many painful memories.

This was to be the first encounter since the divorce. This was also the first meeting with the former in-laws. It would be the first time that the reality (and personal shame) of divorce would be blatantly public. It was a lot to think about in a five-hour drive. More than fifteen years of life were being rehashed all the way. The ex-spouse made the necessary mental preparations: no crying, no trying to win back, approach the situation with grace, civility, and dignity.

The ex-spouse entered the church and sat towards the rear opposite the family side. Fifteen minutes before the ceremony, the former in-laws spotted the spouse sitting alone. They came over and begged her to sit with the family. They made it very evident that the ex-spouse's place was with the family. In later reflection and questioning, she would ask if they had been that vocal when their relative was deciding on divorce? Did they mention the positive aspects of the marriage, or the goodness of the relationship, or were they parties to the deliberations to divorce? One sister teared at the thought of the ex-spouse sitting alone away from the family. Did she cry when the divorce was announced?

The spouses met in the family section. Very few words were exchanged. A simple embrace occurred. After the burial, she went to the reception but left very quickly feeling very out of place. The exes never saw each other again. The drive home was an emotional roller coaster ride. For five hours the ex-spouse was cooped up in an automobile with thousands of voices and belittling memories. The tears were as unending and forceful as the drizzling rain.

> I should have known better than to go. That was the reality of our marriage . . . me always doing for the other. I remember one birthday when my spouse gave me a little plastic Mickey Mouse with a broken arm. There was a laugh as he told our friends that he could give me anything. He said that I liked stupid shit like that. I thought that my going to the funeral would show my love once again. Can't you see that I still love you? It was a waste of time. My in-laws, those hypocrites, did they ever tell him that divorce was not a good decision or that at least we should've talked about it? I hate myself for debasing myself once again. I hate the civility where he takes no blame for his actions. His cop-outs. I thought that when my parents die, I would call. Not anymore. I am not playing his stupid game. He chose this divorce. He can live with the consequences. I hate him.

The ENCOUNTER stage had begun.

FUTURE

"Am I blue?"

Divorce is never a pleasant experience. It leaves its scar on the couple for years to come. Life would be much easier for everyone if the stages had definite beginnings and ends. The stages, however, are simply categories which attempt to name the periods which follow a divorce. They cannot enumerate or classify the multitude of experiences or feelings that emerge during those stages. They cannot predict when those feelings will manifest themselves and take their toll on the human person. The stages simply categorize different shifts in the movement of divorce. Divorce, with its termination of marriage, leaves two people to sort out "what went wrong" for many years to come. Even when both parties have moved on with life, perhaps even with other partners, the memories of a marriage and its termination linger sometimes with unpleasant recollections.

The FUTURE stage is the one which has to be forged by the participants. Both must decide the amount of healing they desire in their life. Both must live with the consequences of their actions since the divorce. Each party must seek healing and gradually move away from the options of reconciliation at all costs or revenge at every angle. The FUTURE stage looks towards healing and acceptance. If those two aspects are not the goal of the FUTURE stage, then chaos will continue for a long time.

The FUTURE stage acknowledges that there is a great possibility that the two ex-spouses may have to face each other in public once again but at a much later date. The FUTURE stage admits, that though the marriage is over, the relationship is unending. It foresees a moment in time when the parties have to look each other squarely in the eye without the desire to attack. It looks for an inner peace within the partners illustrating that both have admitted to the mistake of the marriage. Inner peace occurs when there is an open honesty which reveals to each the culpability of insensitivity. True inner peace comes when both can admit to mistakes in the relationship without having to blame the other.

The FUTURE stage acknowledges that life has continued without the other spouse. It does not necessarily bring inner peace or obvious healing. The FUTURE stage is one which points to the reality that there is a very high probability that the two will again see each other; therefore, healing and preparation must begin immediately after that first initial encounter if not sooner. The FUTURE stage does not look to address any marital issues. It does not seek the well being or settling of leftover affairs from the marriage. The FUTURE stage quite simply states in the meeting face to face, "This was my spouse."

The feelings and emotions, which may evolve from this meeting, are not as severe as initial ones. Naturally, there will be some tension, but it is a reserved tension controlled in public. Nonetheless, it is never an easy meeting. The memories of the past are simply too strong. Even if the meeting occurs after many years, the feelings are still strong enough to evoke uneasiness. What do you say after hello?

This is the person you once wished dead. This is the person you loved once. This is the parent of your child. This is the one who kissed you. This is the one who shared your bed. This is the person who once held the moon. This is the one who sang you love songs. This is the person who cheated on you. This is the person who hated you. This is the person who lied. This is the person you cheated on and to whom you lied. This was your spouse.

I remember watching one former couple during a funeral. We were at the cemetery. This couple had gone through a horrendous marriage with abuse of all kinds. They had finally separated and divorced. It was a bitter violent divorce just like the marriage. The woman's father died. At the graveside, she stood with her new husband, married for about five years. He was good to her. She loved him deeply. After the service he held their little girl's hand as they looked upon the casket in the ground.

The woman cried. Her daddy was dead. Her first husband had attended the funeral as well. He had known the deceased for the length of the previous marriage. They had been friends, too. The deceased was a likeable man, friendly and out-going. Without thinking twice, the first husband went up to his ex-wife and put his arms around her waist. Instinctively, she turned toward him and buried her face and tears in his chest. In his chest was the safety she had known long ago and needed now.

I remember watching fascinated by the intimacy which the couple was still capable of displaying after all of their fighting. She had turned to the man who knew her pain and joy in ways the current husband could never touch. Although never mentioned publicly, the awesome power of forgiveness humbled the bystanders.

The FUTURE stage understands that not everyone heals at the same rate. It foresees the possible problems which may arise. It even predicts the stilted confrontation or conversation which may occur. The FUTURE stage, however, is also a stage of promise and hope. It does desire the healing nature of life. The FUTURE stage is foreshadowed in the feelings and emotions of the ENCOUNTER stage, thus preparing the individuals so that they might have their life put together before they face each other again. The FUTURE stage waits in the wings allowing time to heal as many wounds as it can and making dutiful preparation for the encounter in the future. I recall a woman telling me how her spouse had hurt her.

> It hurts my heart. After seeing him that first time, I told myself that I would never leave myself that vulnerable again. He repeated his well wishes for me, but they came up hollow. Driving to my home from that meeting I heard an old song on the radio with some lyric asking me: "Am I blue?" I live in the tension of wanting to see him again and never wanting to see him. I want him to hurt as I hurt. I want to know if he misses me too. Is he ever blue? I know that I have to face him at least one more time in my life . . . I hate the waiting. I hope I have the strength to love myself enough to get through it . . . whatever that means. I suppose *I am blue.*

The FUTURE stage has not yet begun.

The stages—Reaction, Truth, Encounter, and Future—highlight the phases which have to occur in the great majority of divorce cases. They point to the pain which will have to be encountered as emotions and feelings change but take center stage in each phase. They are also the shining reminders that divorce does not kill a relationship. Divorce, in its own way, extends the relationship until the question of healing is confronted honestly.

The stages overlap with each other providing fodder for the relationship to play out in positive or negative ways. The stages are not hard and fast. Their flexibility allows for the emotions and feelings to control the evolving situations. The encounter with an ex-spouse is always a meeting teeming with past memories and past pain. They do not have to be encounters of future painful memories. The stages exist to remind us of the pitfalls and dangers which lie ahead after the divorce is final.

CASE STUDY

The couple had reached the end of their marital relationship. The marriage had died years ago; it just lacked the final sword. Although both parties were very aware of the problems in the relationship, they chose not to address them. There was much bickering and arguing over the slightest silliest issues. They were tired of being together. They were like two individuals living separate lives under one roof. The vows had long since been forgotten. Theirs was a marriage in name.

The husband could never understand what went wrong. He refused to believe that his spouse did not love him. Despite the numerous problems, un-communicated expectations, and general disgust in being with each other, the husband blindly believed that people stay married. Divorce for him was not an option.

Once in a very heated discussion, the husband began to enumerate the faults of his spouse. He was angry at the way he was treated. He was sore at not being loved, for always having to cater to his spouse. All he desired was for his spouse to care about him. He wanted to know that when he was talking the spouse was listening instead of working on the computer. He wanted to know that he was more important than the spouse's work outside the home. He wanted to feel that his spouse loved him for who he was and not for something she wanted him to be. He wanted to be the most important person in the life of his spouse rather than relegated to the position of housemate. He wanted to know that he was more important in his spouse's life than any of their mutual friends. He wanted to know that he was loved as any brother or sister in his spouse's family. He wanted to be the husband.

The spouse too had desires. She wanted a husband who was willing to offer more companionship instead of being driven by work. The spouse wanted a mate who would not be so drawn to the needs of his parents. The spouse wanted the freedom to have other friends separate from the husband. She wanted the husband to be a more active participant in the doings and outings of the in-laws. The spouse wanted the husband to play a larger role in the extended family picture.

In the heated discussion, nothing was settled. The night of the announcement of the divorce the spouse began.

Since you don't like the way I treat you, I don't think you should have to put up with it anymore . . .

What, what are you saying?

Since I am all those things which you do not like maybe we shouldn't be together.

You don't want me?

I have treated you badly . . . We should separate.

You don't want me?

We're just hurting each other now.

The husband left, but before he got to the door he turned to the spouse crying,

You don't love me?

No . . . I love you but not like before . . . Take care of yourself!

I love you . . . why are you doing this?

Take care of yourself!

After several conversations seeking some type of understanding as to why the divorce occurred, the spouse would always end the conversation with, "Take care of yourself." This was the catch phrase she had learned to pat herself on the back with civility and concern while casting aside the relationship. This was a planned phrase as hollow as a bottom-less pit. It lacked the simple courtesies the marriage lacked. This phrase echoes Pilate's washing of hands before he abandons Jesus to be crucified. This phrase had all the sincerity of seeing a homeless beggar and telling him to "keep warm and well fed" (Jas 2:15–17). This phrase highlights the sinfulness of sounding sincere but being mean.

On reflection, the husband began to understand the method by which he was dismissed. His spouse had chosen to accept the blame for everything using the husband's own disagreements as the way out of the marriage. Without any sincerity, she simply agreed to the husband's accusations, to avoid addressing any of the issues. In the best attempt at hypocritical civility, the spouse, choosing to be rid of the husband, simply said, "Take care of yourself!"

The husband was angry. Someone had taught his spouse the phrase and technique in order to get out of the marriage without having to face guilt or remorse. The husband went crazy, blaming every friend and enemy and cursing them in the process.

"TAKE CARE OF YOURSELF!" What in the hell did that mean?

The phrase was as phony as the vows. It allowed the marriage to die with the same lies by which it had been lived. Simultaneously, it spoke of the reality of marriage for the husband. For all of the years in the marriage, he had taken care of himself.

PASTORAL REFLECTION

A beautiful story in the Gospel of John chapter 11 shows us the humanity of Jesus most movingly. Jesus' friend Lazarus dies. This story, so often quoted and cited in funerals, focuses on the Jesus' tears crying for someone he loves. This story is rich in the stages of Christian grief and reflection. It is the story of Christianity crying with the Lord and rejoicing in the foreshadowing of a glorious resurrection.

The story, abundant in imagery, full of hope, teaches us how grief itself moves through different stages. The beauty of the Lazarus story is that it is not about Lazarus at all. This story is the mirror we peer into when uncovering our emotions and feelings, as grief becomes a reality in our lives.

The first stage is a wonderful prayer that has been uttered by every faithful Christian when confronted with a situation that does not make any sense. Martha and Mary both ask the Lord in a simple prayer: "Where were you?" How many times have those words been uttered by our lips? How many times from the agonizing hurt of divorce have we asked the Lord where he was without realizing he had never been truly included in the beginning? How many times in deep questioning have we approached the Lord whom we love with that gnawing question of why has this happened?

Jesus' response to Martha is the climax of his teaching. He reminds her that he is the Resurrection and the Life. Jesus then poses to her a question which every Christian has to answer. Jesus asks her if she believes that he is the resurrection and life. Martha's response is the quintessential reply of faith. She states that she has come to believe that he is the Messiah. Martha's response indicates her progression of faith. When she considers all of the blessings she has received with Jesus, she can state definitively: "I have come to believe." When she looks back in honest reflection she can see that the Lord has walked with her at all moments of her life, however difficult. Knowing his presence in her heart, she can realize his love for her. In her discernment and reflection she has come to believe because she can recognize the footprints of God in her life.

This first stage is vitally important in any crisis situation especially divorce. We beg God for an answer, and the Lord tells us that he is the Resurrection and the Life. He desires to hear from our own lips that we have come to believe because we can recognize that he has walked with us in even the darkest moments of our life. In the bleakest moment of Martha's life, she can still reflect on the fact that God has loved her in the past; therefore, he will love her into a future she cannot see.

The second stage is a very tender one. It is the moment when Jesus stands before the tomb of his friend and cries. He is an adult man in touch with his grief and not ashamed by any cultural taboos or traditions against crying. Jesus had just told Martha and Mary of his own majesty, yet he cries from the depth of his heart because he hurts. This relationship was not expected to have ended this way. Death has come and taken from Jesus the one whom he loves. Rumors abound as bystanders begin to criticize Jesus.

The rumors hurt. They are said callously as if Jesus were not present to hear them. There is very little respect for his feelings. The bystanders are filled with opinions and not shy about expressing them to anyone who will listen. They wonder aloud about Jesus' power and could care less about his grief.

The beauty of this scene is found in the salty tears streaming from the Son of Mary. At this point, there is no shame in crying for his friend. He teaches us that grief demands that we be honest with our hurting feelings. He shows us that we can find comfort without shame in the grace of human tears. He reminds us that bystanders (and family) always have opinions but that those opinions are miniscule to non-existent when compared with the richness of our tears.

The third stage is the prayer of Jesus. It is a powerful reminder to all believers of his tenderness. His relationship with his Father is so intimate that now he stands before the powers and stench of death. He reminds his Father of the love between them, and his prayer is prayed that the people might come to believe.

This prayer is a constant reminder of the Lord's thirst for our belief. It shows us his eternal intercession on our behalf. It illustrates that God knows our weaknesses, our moments of disbelief. This prayer of Jesus is the sign that the situations we perceive as hopeless and dead are rendered graced as the Lord intercedes on our behalf. The pain of grief (divorce), the moments which cannot be avoided (encountering the "ex"), the feelings and emotions which entomb us, are all shattered as we hear the Lord plead for our belief.

The fourth stage is the most demanding. The moment when Jesus calls Lazarus out of the tomb is when grief is transformed into joy. It is the moment of healing and belief. It is the time when Lazarus encounters life again; that which was dead is alive again. It is the sign of a new beginning, a literal resurrection. It is the stage which points to the future. It is the moment when Jesus teaches that if resurrection is to occur then Lazarus must be unbound and set free.

All encounters with Jesus look toward healing. After the devastation (death) of divorce, the human person cries for healing. Through all of the stages in every facet of rage, the soul still desires a peace that it might have life again and life in abundance (John 10:10). In the quiet moments of reflection, any wounded human being will search for inner peace (Ps 130:6). The answer is found in the last stage of this story. Jesus tells the bystanders that Lazarus must be unbound in order to experience freedom.

His words do not change with the grieving of today. The divorced seek peace. They desire a life free from the abusive relationship they lived.

They seek a moment in their future which will tell them that life does continue and that resurrection is not limited to physical death. They look for a resurrection of their self-worth.

In this last stage, Jesus teaches that revenge can never provide an adequate response to any grief. No matter what has occurred in the marriage or its subsequent divorce, Jesus says to unbind it, and let it go free. Those memories, which come back to haunt, or the anger, which gnaws like a ravenous rat, have to be unbound so that the divorced might walk free. To live in the past, to nurse harsh memories, and to harbor the feelings of revenge seal the tomb of people's lives. Jesus has called his children to peace (1 Cor 7:15c) and has taught us once again that letting go of past hurts is the only way to live fruitfully in the future.

Living in the past (memories, arguments, fights, trials) does not affect an ex-spouse. It affects only the one living in the past. Jesus is the God of the Present. It is in the here and now that he speaks this Gospel reminding us that his tears were for his friend. His miracle was that his friend might have life again. He has cried tears before the tombs in which we have been interred. Sincere friends have pleaded with him on our behalf: Lord the one whom you love has died (divorced). Come and see where he lay. The Lord in the splendor of his gentleness has cried because of the human suffering which has taken place. Out of love for his friend (us), Jesus has prayed us out of the darkness. New life rich in freedom is born of letting go.

The couple is stuck in the tomb of their self-righteousness. The wife found a convenient way not to have to address the separation. She used a simple phrase wrapped in insincerity to negate feelings and emotions. Where did this spouse learn this technique? Who told her to keep that line and not waver? It was just another example of the lack of care for the husband's feelings. The husband should not be so shocked because if an honest reflection had been done, it is more than likely that this pattern existed throughout the marriage. Why should the divorce be different?

The husband has focused on the phrase ("take care of yourself") in order to nurse his rage. He refuses to admit to the problems which existed in the marriage. He lives in some fairy-tale illusion that divorce does not occur. He cannot see his own culpability even though he admits it was a marriage in name only. He believes that if they had stayed together things would have worked out without ever finding out what needed repairing.

Jesus teaches in the story of Lazarus' death and resurrection that crises have their own movements before healing can occur. Time is required. Faith is necessary. Healing is not some wishbone that can be grabbed by the strongest or most aggressive person. Healing demands openness to one's tears and God's Word. Healing negates all revenge as it looks to the future. Healing understands that a new life is possible even when all seems lost. Jesus, human enough to cry and loving enough to pray, reminds us that in the darkest moment of life he is the Resurrection and the Life. Do you believe this?

PRAYER OF PRESENCE

Lord I tried to hide myself
from me,
from you.
I hurt and cried.
I bled inside.

Lord, I tried to hide
my wound,
my pain.
I could not see you.
I could not see me.

Lord, I tried to hide.
Your love warmed me.
Your hands touched me.
Your cross
saved me.

6

Ass Warts

FEELINGS ARISING FROM A divorce are overwhelming. Without discriminating, feelings surging from a divorce attack the human psyche diverting and consuming the entire thought process serendipitously. Sometimes a television program, a thought, a scene in a movie, or a picture recalls the spouse. Sometimes music in the mall, a familiar meal, or a quiet pensive moment interrupts the day with memories. Sometimes it's just a song. Then it happens.

The reality of being divorced overcomes all other aspects of life, and the wound that was supposed to be healed is ripped open to bleed for all to see. Divorcing partners manage the physical environment, juggling all the complexities of life, family, and work, yet a simple melody can reduce a person to tears. The depth of the hurt, however, is known only to the divorced. Unexpectedly, the physical environment gives way to the raging effusion of memories producing a torrent of tears and rage, anger and hurt, fear and loneliness. The eruption of memories fused with the rush of emotions devastates the tranquility sought in life.

Those feelings, however, lacking any moral value, can control or influence actions and behavior. Feelings have a tremendous power to influence our thoughts and actions in ways and means that, at times, we do not even notice. Feelings attempt to placate the wounded heart trying to heal itself in an unhealthy emotional equation. Feelings trying to ameliorate wounded memories pull from an unqualified resource. Feelings attempt to be the salve of the hurt memory, yet they lack the objectivity needed in order to continue on with a healthy life.

Everything about life reminds us all that life is continuous. Everything around us teaches us that life is bigger than divorce and its lasting hurt. Everything around us reminds us that we are still graced people called to bask in the reality of the love of God. Our feelings, however, can sometimes get stuck and focused on one hurting area to the exclusion of the entirety of life and its wholeness (*i.e.,* holiness). We become blind to the goodness of the grace of God surrounding us. The hurt of divorce is so vast and deep, it becomes difficult to behold the beauty of God all around us shouting to us that we may be healed. We cannot see even the beauty of the divine image God has put within us, so great is guilt or shame.

Failure to recognize feelings deep within us can lead to self-doubt, anger, rage, and even self-destructive behavior. Feelings in one way or another must be addressed. If feelings are not addressed, they will fester and grow, finding inappropriate ways of manifesting themselves. Inappropriate ways have no public bounds. The feelings will manifest themselves publicly, not caring who is present as a witness, or privately, forcing one to face very real unpleasant realities.

Some people try to hide their feelings even from themselves, suppressing the feelings until like a pressure cooker they rise to the surface and explode in rage, strokes, anger, or heart/ health problems. Feelings cannot be hidden in some unseen vessel deep within us so that we do not have to face their tough consequences. They cannot be suppressed because they will seek an outlet, be it physical, spiritual, psychological, sexual, or emotional. Feelings will seek an outlet either healthy or dangerous.

Truth be known, suppressed feelings affect every part of our being. They have the power to make one physically ill. Invisible feelings affect the visible physical body. As St. Paul states to the Corinthians, "The eye cannot say to the hand, I have no need of you" (1 Cor 12:21). Feelings often determine physical health because of the interlocking connectedness between physical health and feelings. The result can be devastating.

Feelings by their very nature demand to be acknowledged and recognized for their value and worth as part of the person's psyche. Feelings need to be addressed for what they contribute to understanding the environment of laughter and joy, sadness and grief. The more difficult reality is that one must seek out the roots of feelings and why they are recurring. It is a difficult search because the truth can be frightening. The truth is located when the roots are shaken clean from the soil of divorce and broken relationship. Without any assignation of blame or culpability, the roots of feelings arising from divorce have very little to do with the ex-spouse. The most frightening truth is that both spouses are forced to look at him or herself.

When a couple enters into a marital relationship, they bring to it the understanding of marriages they witnessed as they were growing up. They do not come into the relationship *tabula rasa* (*i.e.,* clean slate). They are filled with all of the prejudices about life and marriage that they have experienced in their families. No one enters into a pure and pristine relationship. Relationships are filled with all of the diseases, excuses, or limitations of family life.

Diseases like alcoholism, sexism, racism, materialism, lack of communication, family cycles, games and roles affect each person in the relationship. It is impossible to disclose all of the factors which have formed us before a marriage occurs, though the dating period should be the time to discover what has basically formed the other person. The dating period should explore the feelings of each person so as to reduce relational surprises and to blend differences into similarities.

It is, however, within formational factors that our feelings about life, and, consequently, marriage, are bred and cultivated. Those feelings are brought into the relationship of marriage. A healthy marriage calls into conversion the diseased aspects of family and seeks the grace of blending the positive aspects of two people to form one flesh. An unhealthy marriage refuses any conversion and allows the diseases to fester and germinate. Divorce will illuminate those roots exposing the sensitivity in which a person has been raised. Divorce will expose the tragic reality of what makes us cry when the relationship terminates.

Although the natural reaction when divorce occurs is to focus on the ex-spouse and his or her peccadilloes, the raw feelings in the moment of divorce have everything to do with one's life history and not the sinful actions of one who supposedly loved and then did not. How divorce is fleshed out depends greatly on how far a person has gone beyond the family idols worshipped over the years. Moving beyond divorce depends upon the extent to which one has removed the family masks or roles we have been taught to wear in order to hide our real selves.

Although studies in grief will show different stages for an individual to move beyond the initial pain, the pain of divorce, like a cancer, erupts at different moments, within different seasons, and with the queerest of memories, sometimes real and sometimes misremembered. The pain knows no time limit and cannot be reduced by a specific healing time. There is no scheduled hour for pain's removal from the psyche. Pain lacks a predetermined formula for healing *(sanatio).*

Pain may become dormant for a period, but it is certainly not dead. Sleeping comfortably in the recesses of the mind without waking for some time, pain requires very little to arouse the memories of marriage and divorce, allowing the pain to surface even to the point of tears. Although life may have advanced and healing appears complete, very often apparent healing is simply a façade waiting to be exposed and revived. A divorced person may find him-or herself for no reason whatsoever alone in grief months and even years later. The hurt can be as intense as the first moment of the actual separation.

Our language speaks of "for no reason whatsoever," but it is a sad fact the tears streaming much later on come for many reasons, from many roots, and many sources. The divorced knows only too well the deep reason for the tears. Grieving reminds the divorced couple that no matter how far he or she has advanced in life or moved on, divorce has been a very painful chapter which everyone would erase if possible. Divorce in anyone's history is the constant reminder of not being loved and of being a human failure. It is an ever-present image of human loss.

The management of our feelings is not an easy task. Because of the painful reality of breaking up and starting over, a person may be given over to the obsession about what has occurred. Obsessing about the painful memories has more than once caused a person to live and dwell in the land of "what if I had" and "if I could change one thing." Any time anyone moves into the non-reality of life, it is a dangerous negation of what is. It is a path laced with devastating wolfish memories ready to devour the calm in one's life. Obsessing can lead one down the road of serious depression. When feelings begin to overwhelm the reality of life, a person places him-herself in an imaginary world.

Like King Saul conjuring up Samuel from the dead with the help of the witch of Endor, the imaginary laced with one's feelings conjures up old memories, old arguments, old anger, old good times, and old hate (1 Sam 28:7–14). Sparked by the most insignificant memory from a song, or a movie, a haunt, a familiar phrase, or even a smell, the power of feelings aids the divorced to conjure up from nowhere the very person from whom he/she is divorced. Without ever being physically present, the ex-spouse is very present. It is not uncommon for the divorced to carry on imaginary arguments all over again in the mind as if they were actually talking to the one whom they hate, as if they could actually win one last battle, as if they had the actual last word, years later.

In spiritual direction, there is an underlying tenet, which teaches the nature of God's presence. In the greatest absence, there is the greatest presence. This faith statement exemplifies the eternal presence of God's love when we least expect it. It is a beautiful statement of God's love for us. Conversely and not in a very positive light, a divorced person triggered by the feelings stirred from a memory (song, movie, place, smell, etc.) lives the same statement. In the greatest absence of the divorced ex-spouse, there is the greatest presence of the divorced ex-spouse.

With the physical absence of the ex-spouse, one's feelings have a free-for-all in the rage against the non-existent. Tears flow involuntarily. Memories run amok. Anger surges. The mind envisions the devil incarnate. Often a strong bitterness begins to fester within the soul at odds with Christian virtue but festering nonetheless. As more feelings arise and more memories strum the imaginary life in the mind, bitterness can become an obsession.

A divorced person reeling in anger about life and the reality of divorce may obsess about many areas which because of the divorce have no meaning. The divorced may obsess about the whereabouts of the ex-spouse. Who are they with now? Are they thinking of me? Are we going to reconcile? What about my life? The obsession grows ultimately culminating into the only question that matters at all: "Did you ever love me?"

The unanswerable question born of pain and grief is the only question seeking an honest answer, and, in divorce, this is the only question which will fulfill the marriage promise until death do us part. The question "Did you ever love me?" is the nail mark in the broken marriage. It is the eternal external wound shaping the rest of life. Bury it. Hide it. Tell yourself you have gone beyond it. That question desires an answer that will satisfy the subsequent and real question: "Then what happened?"

Divorce showcases the inability to resolve those questions ("Did you ever love me; then what happened?") to any type of satisfaction. Even though a logical reasonable answer might be attained, the answer will never be enough to satisfy the feelings. Feelings will always be the embers of the divorce that when stoked will ignite the bonfire of tears, anger, or rage. It is always the goal to go beyond the pain and hurt, but when the focus on the memories becomes a consistent pattern in one's life, there is a great danger that the pattern of thought becomes an obsession.

The obsession, the constant asking of questions which have absolutely no answer, roots itself in a fear of loneliness coated in anger at the ex-spouse and eventually at oneself. The obsession with having to start over in every relational aspect of life can be so threatening that at that moment, it can consume one's entire life. Obsession becomes consumption.

Consumption, the constant fixation on the past in an attempt to rectify the present, is the most unhealthy situation any divorced person can enter. When memories filled with anger, or rage consume a person's life to the point of obscuring reality, then they are given over to a more difficult life condemned to fighting past ghosts, phantoms of marriage difficulties. Living in the past is a dangerous place of memory, for it fails to recognize that those days are over. Life has gone beyond the old arguments. Life does not recognize who won and who lost.

The present reality knows no solution from the past. The present could care less about past joys and tears. The present looks to tomorrow for a new life. Consumption, on the other hand, forces the divorced to live in the shadows and tears of times gone by. Memories can consume a person to the point of depression, physical and psychological. That unanswerable question ("Did you ever love me?") can be consuming as it attempts to re-live the past moments looking for clues and signs as to why the break-up occurred. The subsequent question ("Then what happened?") raises an even deeper question, "then why don't you love me now?" exasperating the hurt beyond balm.

When a divorcing person becomes consumed with trying to rectify the impossible, life becomes a series of frustrations, with losses at every corner, tears at every juncture. Consumption, laced at times with painful memories of being enamored once and hated, now is even more devastating for the one living the divorced reality. Every song, every television show on relationships, every article about life and love can become a focal point for the consumption to fester into negative and painful moments of tears resulting in the questioning even of the value of life itself.

Consumption will lead depressed persons to moments of suicidal thoughts, the rock bottom conclusion that maybe even God does not love them. It is the moment of darkness, the primal void of the waters of chaos (Gen 1:1). The divorced person, consumed by memories, echoes the prayer of the psalmist, "My only friend is darkness" (Ps 88).

Rock bottom is a difficult place to live. The choices are not many. The options provide for life or death. There is a shadowy third option which many divorced people choose to their own detriment until they actually realize that there are only two options, life or death. The third option is to live as a walking living dead person. Living dead persons choose to live in the here and now passing time, but to dwell mentally in the past. They reek of past dead moments. They walk and breathe, but they smell of a dead marriage. It is as if they choose to carry a huge trash bag of marriage memories with them, lugging it from place to place, person to person. At work, it is with them. At home, it is with them. At play, it is with them.

It is always the hope that a living dead person will awake to the reality that life has more to offer. It is the prayer of their friends that they will see the baggage they carry and throw it off that they might live more freely and unburdened, but only the walking living dead person can actually make that decision.

When one reaches rock bottom, if the depression is great, then sometimes the suicidal route is chosen. Not seeing the way out the divorcing find the darkness too great. Only the Lord, who is light from light, has the ability to caress that soul eternally.

In a beautiful passage from the letter to the Christians in Rome (Rom 8), St. Paul writes that there are moments in our life when things are so oppressive in our lives that we do not know even how to pray. He was speaking of his own life. This great theologian, this Apostle to the Gentiles called by God to be the Other Apostle (Gal 2:16), who gave the Church its crux of theology, writes of his own dark moment. He states that in those moments when we do not know how to access God, when we cannot hear the Lord God's voice or feel his presence, that the Holy Spirit who lives within us intercedes to the Father on our behalf (Rom 8:26).

The Holy Spirit begs for us, praying to the Father in a language beyond human speech "with sighs too deep for words." St. Paul knew that in our faith lives there are also the moments of great darkness, but because of our baptism, the Holy Spirit shoots from us like a spring of flowing water to the eternal Father that we might have life and life in abundance (John 10:10). When a person hits rock bottom after a divorce, and the decision is life or death, the Holy Spirit, struggling against all of our memories of anger and rage, of hurt and deceit, of abuse (physical, verbal, emotional, sexual, psychological, or spiritual), intercedes for us beyond our imaginings.

It is the Holy Spirit living and dwelling in the temple of our lives who breathes and hovers over the waters of our chaos that we might be re-created (Gen 1:1). The moment at rock bottom is when the Holy Spirit using all of the divine gifts reminds us that where sin abounds grace abounds in abundance (Rom 5:20). It is the Spirit shaping us and praying for us that we might see once again the beauty of the Divine Image living within us. It is the Holy Spirit calling us once more to choose life.

Life, however, because of divorce, necessitates an entire re-definition. All of life is now viewed by divorced eyes. All events, even the most routine ones, are now re-defined from a new perspective, a divorced one. At the core of all re-definition is the re-defining of oneself. For so many years, months, even days, the divorced person has been defined as part of a couple. Almost like an appendage, the person has lost some of his or her own identity having been seen always as a part of the other spouse. The mixture of persons that formed a couple affected every part of the married person's life.

All of the elements which characterized the couple who loved each other (the physical, psychological, spiritual, sexual, or material) now cry to be re-defined as belonging to separate individuals again. Re-definition is not an easy task. One cannot be re-defined back to the person he/she was before the relationship. Individuality has been compromised by the marriage relationship. A person's own personal beliefs, what they hold as their own thoughts even about their own individuality, have been shaped and re-shaped, lauded and criticized, praised and abased by the marriage relationship.

Redefinition becomes a time-consuming process of trying to understand "who I am" as a single human being. It is an arduous and painful adventure demanding the individual to understand the deepest recesses of the heart because nothing of life is the same. Redefinition demands that the individual's life has absolutely nothing to do with the life of the previous spouse. Even when children are involved, divorced persons must limit and restrict their lives only to the children and their wellbeing and not to the life of the previous spouse. The temptation to regulate and opine about the other is so strong that it can lead a divorced couple to barbaric behavior, stirring up emotions spiced with hate without much regard for anyone around them.

Redefinition teaches a person simple human behavior all over again. Eating, sleeping, working, laughing, crying, and dating are actions which have to be re-defined with a new perspective. Things once taken for granted by the whole populace become events that have new meaning for a wounded now single person. Actions require a redefining of thought as well. Writing a check, planning a vacation, making the bed, going to a movie, going out to eat, signing one's name are but a few of the moments which have to be redefined by both parties. The simplest of tasks require a whole new thought process, reminding the divorced they are single. Simple tasks evoke tears. A re-interpretation has to occur.

Redefinition is the next step in the grieving process. A death has occurred. The death of the marriage now calls for a redefining of personhood. Through all the tears, emotions, and feelings, divorced persons have to begin the process and work of defining their own being. Who am I without the other person? How is my life defined now as a single person? How do I perform simple human actions alone?

Redefinition has to occur in order to restore sanity and life into an ordered life. Redefinition liberates the person from the unhealthy lived reality of anger and obsession. Obsession, which dominated the soul, loses its significance as simple human tasks are redefined into single personhood.

Naturally, there will be the pitfalls of memory and the tears of past hurts that will creep into one's life causing setbacks in the recovery process of re-defining. They can be as devastating as the initial shock of the divorce eliciting the same intensity of tears and anger. Re-defining simple tasks will lose intensity with time. Keeping focused on redefining life without the other person is essential to a healthy living; it must become a daily routine.

Anger is a very powerful emotion which determines many of our actions. It must be channeled into positive energy. Once anger becomes an obsession, it becomes that much more uncontrollable. Anger, however, always needs to be examined by the toll it is taking on an individual. How does anger affect the emotional stability of everyday living? When anger becomes an obsession rooted in hatred, it is self-destructive. Neither anger or hatred has any effect on the other spouse. They simply consume the angry hater.

The way out of this cycle has its basis in the re-definition of the human. As simple as it sounds, simple human living, the continuing on with daily routine, will be the liberating factor in one's divorced life. Redefining will teach that he or she were never created in the image of the ex-spouse, but that they were created in the image of a loving God (Gen 1:27). What the pain of divorce attempts to deceive, re-definition uncovers in the light of truth (John 3:20).

CASE STUDY

The couple had been together for seventeen years and 331 days. The marriage had gone through so many different stages that it had experienced the extremes of all emotions. Their communication had had its strongest moments and gradually waned for lack of use into the abysmal. They continually paraded a facade of love to themselves, their friends, and their acquaintances. In many aspects they had reached a point in their married life when toleration was normative. Lovemaking and sexual intimacies had become a chore at times and simply a release at others.

At some level they both knew that they did love each other, but it had become more difficult to reach that level. The sadness lay in the trying to discover the love, for over time, they had dug a deeper and deeper hole hiding the intimate level of genuine selfless love to themselves. Distance became a major player in their communication—verbally, emotionally, psychologically, sexually, and spiritually. As they distanced from each other, they lived the lie until death do us part. If the truth be known, the marriage had died, but they had not parted.

On the surface the divorce seemed amicable, but the deep resentments, which had festered over the years, had, like a cancer, spread throughout one of the spouses to the point that the anger became all-consuming. It was a brutal departure for the both of them. There was only one bitter phone call demanding to know if a third party were involved. The call was met with such a harsh coldness, an attitude of "none of your business," that it simply stoked the fires of doubt and blame on the part of the questioner. As the questions bred more questions, the pain of divorce matured into a hatred of marriage, the spouse, oneself, and life itself. The questioner reached the suicidal point of divorce where death is perceived as a better option than living.

All the questions of "how could this happen to me, why did this happen, who is the other person(s), am I that repugnant?" surfaced into the mental anguish of the spouse as obsession became the norm. The spouse, now separated, obsessed over the past years of good times and bad, of fidelity and infidelities, of love and hate, of richness and poverty. Love was evaluated from both viewpoints: desiring the best for the other person, and working with all that one is to provide the best for the other person. The marriage definitely came up lacking. It was difficult to pinpoint where the marriage had died, but there were definite moments that screamed for attention. Hindsight revealed that those screams went unheard and unattended.

The divorce was fast. Separation was brutal. There were few harsh words, but the feelings were intense and thick. Tears gushed forth from both sides. As the husband initiated the separation, hurting from his heart to the point that he could not even verbalize the words "I want out," the other agreed without realizing the anger and hurt which had taken up residence in her heart. That anger and hurt nascent in the soul would blossom into an uncontrollable obsession leading to a consuming vengeance: *the mistaken evil desire to want the other person to hurt as much as I do.*

The obsession of the wife became all-consuming. There was not one day that the "ex" did not think of or curse the husband. There was very little to almost no physical contact once the separation occurred. Over a period of almost five years, there was but one accusatory phone call and a family funeral where there was any contact at all. After that, there was no communication at all. Nevertheless, the wife's obsession became overwhelming. They lived hundreds of miles apart, but the memories were always very present, eating at the mind and enveloping the heart-strings of the one spouse until many lines of thought became blurred and indistinguishable.

The devastated spouse, somewhere in the miasma of pain and memory, began to beg God for help. The quest for justice was enormous. The civil divorce was entirely amicable, but in the depths of the soul, the obsessed spouse began to cry to the heavens of her hurt. The human cry of tears became a mental cry of anguish. She could never make things right in the mind. The loneliness was profound. The tears became a living hell.

The spouse echoed and prayed the Psalm feeling and believing that "my only friend is darkness" (Ps 88). The mental breakdown, always graced in the salt of tears and too many times in an alcohol depressant, was so real and so private that the spouse crossed over into the unimaginable. It was not justice she sought. The obsession cried for vengeance: *the misdirected notion and heartfelt desire that the other person hurt and, in this case, emotionally.* Vengeance reached the mental point of wishful desire where if the spouse were God then the "ex" would be annihilated, erased from the book of life. The problem with obsession is that it is never sated. Even if annihilation had occurred, the anger would still not subside.

In private meditation, the obsessed spouse began to walk down a road of mental chaos. Believing the saying whose sins you retain they are retained, the spouse began to think about the entire system of justice (John 20:23b). Knowing in the depths of the heart that human justice is simply human, the spouse, full of tears, full of vengeance, wandered into the mental realm of fantasy.

"I wonder about how courts really work. I know that God loves me, and God loves my "ex." I know separation and divorce occurred, but I also know that justice was not done. I have been treated as if my feelings were unimportant. My feelings have never been important to him. I know the whole marriage was pretty much lived that way, but my feelings hurt. I feel they have been rendered unimportant even to the point of non-existence. It never matters how I feel, and deep down inside, I know I am not meant to hurt this way. We are divorced, but I still cry for some justice."

The spouse, dabbling in Tarot cards while at the same time going to church, began to meditate without direction. The obsession, blurring any sense of reality, created an illusion of respectability in order that vengeance might find an outlet no matter how erroneous the premise was. Vengeance found its place and dominance in a self-righteousness crying and pleading for justice in this situation.

Although the separation and divorce were final with no expected reconciliation and with everyone fully aware of that fact, there was still an aching hurt which grew into an obsession. The emotionally devastated spouse crying daily, drinking daily, cursing daily, and living in the warped justice of the human mind sought the powers of the mental spirit worlds creating an elaborate system of justice in which to appeal the case in her own mind. Her thinking went as follows:

> There are other courts in which to appeal my case. The first court is the human court of justice which has decided, deliberated, and declared the union over. It does not deal with justice. Its only aim is to separate and dissolve. So I went to other courts for justice.
>
> There is the court of creation. All around us is the world in which we participate, but write off as if we were here first, as if we are the only creation that matters. Everyone knows creation was first. It lives and is governed by the laws of nature. Creation all around us has its own routine. We simply take for granted and actually believe that creation operates under our supervision. It does not.

After a great deal of Pinot Grigio one night, I began to think of my situation. I could feel the anger intensified by the wine and my depression disordering my very thought process. How do you stop the tears once they begin to flow through all of the memories? How do you stop the unending stream of salt water laced with innumerable memories? How do you cry on a piece of paper?

In a moment of deep depression and sadness, I stepped out of this world and walked into a different place. I could hear the voices of the winds. I could see the moon shining over both of us, reflecting its orbital communication with the sun. I felt the gentle caress of moonlight memories and the warmth of sunbeams at the beach and in the park. I could feel the salt of the ocean on my face and the sand between my toes. I knew the wind blew not only on my face, but at this moment, it was blowing through all of my soul. I could feel the hurt of all creation groaning. I knew in the depths of my heart, that I too was a creature.

For a split moment, creation opened its filmy layer of being, and I beheld an even more magnificent place of softness. Seeing softness and beholding nothing, I understood there was an even different court above the court of creation. It was the court of celestial beings. I knew at that moment that if there was the court of celestial beings, then somehow I had access even to the justice of the divine God.

I knelt down on the floor and called upon the winds, north and south, east and west, to hear my case and to see the wrong which had been done to me. In the name of all creation, I cursed my "ex." I asked all of creation to hear me, to judge my case. I asked creation which influences my feelings to see how they had been rendered non-existent. I asked creation to envelop me. Those winds, that sun and moon, that earth, sky, water, and fire which have influenced and touched the core of my being all of my life, I asked to sit in judgment of the treatment I had received. As I made my case, I asked that my ex-spouse hurt as I hurt. My feelings are important to me. As they hurt, I seriously petitioned that my "ex" hurt more.

I could not erase the memory of the celestial court. I, however, relied on the court of creation to hear my appeal. This was no aberration. God has always provided for me. I too am part of that creation. Even though I had never paid attention to its role, I felt very comfortable explaining my case and asking for justice.

The devastated spouse in the warped mental state enhanced by the alcohol consumption intoned inaudible and incomprehensible incantations laced with tears appealing to the powers of creation to curse the other spouse. The mind, filled with images of creational memories, flooded itself with obsession and vengeance and justified the curse in a self-righteous appeal rooted in the hurtful reality of never having feelings honestly communicated. The appeal to the court of creation became a routine with the alcohol and depression. The invocation of a broader vision of justice became a common occurrence, an almost daily practice.

Perhaps if the husband had simply asked about the feelings, then there would have been no curse, no misunderstanding or imaginings of creational and celestial courts. Perhaps a simple checking in on the other, a simple "how are you doing?" might have prevented the craziness of courts and curses. Concern for feelings never occurred, and the resulting madness found its outlet in the absurd.

The husband never knew of the madness or cared to know. He was never concerned for the feelings of the "ex" or her wellbeing. His spouse's feelings and balance, like in the marriage, were never an issue. Why would feelings be an issue in the separation and divorce? It is not that the husband was uncaring in the separation and divorce. It is that he never cared about the feelings of his spouse in the courtship or in marriage. Consequently and obviously, there was never a gracious segue into the separation and divorce. How could there have been?

Being very promiscuous himself, the "ex" ventured into sexual activity after the separation and divorce. He had been unfaithful during the marriage but refused to acknowledge any culpability on his part. He was just glad he was out of a stifling suffocating relationship. He initiated the divorce and was adept at not communicating. The non-communication tactic maintained a safe distance. Non-communication with the "ex" meant non-engaging. Non-engaging ensures not having to deal with any feelings, his or his ex-spouse's.

His sexual promiscuity led him into some type of sexual activity in which he contracted ass warts. Ass warts are hemorrhoids turned inside out. They are very painful, and located inside the rectum, must be removed by searing. It is a very painful procedure in which each wart must be burned off the inside ring of the rectum. The physical pain is excruciating while the bleeding mixed with fecal odor lends itself to all the connotations of unprotected deviant sex lacking in hygienic appropriateness.

One day the devastated spouse was speaking with a mutual friend, Coco, when Coco inadvertently mentioned having seen the other spouse.

As questions and answers were exchanged her friend Coco jokingly asked the devastated spouse if she had been dabbling in black magic.

"No. I do not believe in black magic. I believe in God and in his mercy and justice. God is just."

Coco began to speak of the ass warts situation. There was silence at the other end of the conversation. The still grieving ex-spouse absorbed the information. The court of creation had heard the plea. Creation had had its say. The sentence was ass warts. Ass warts would be the manner in which justice would be administered. "Feel that!" thought the emotionally overwhelmed spouse without the slightest sympathy. "I hope your ass burns. Fuck you!"

The distraught spouse mused about the power of the curses. Pleased with the sentence of ass warts, however, she never ceased cursing the other one. Caught between the feelings of loving and hating, she continued to live in a warped alcoholic misunderstanding of the blend of justice and mercy.

Those sins which you retain are retained. Sad to say, that break-up, which by now should have been satiated with the sentence of ass warts, still cries for justice. Justice will never even have a beginning if communication never takes place. On the part of the devastated spouse, living still in the mixed feelings of hate and love, there is not one day which passes in which the other is not cursed and blessed. Although ass warts were a painful reality, nothing satiates an obsession.

PASTORAL REFLECTION

As physical bodies begin to show the effects of being overwhelmed by painful memories, it is nothing compared to the devastating toll that has occurred to the spiritual body. We are not mechanical robots who simply function in this world. We are human beings created in the Divine Image (Gen 1:27). We are human beings who were formed and fashioned in the wombs of our mothers (Ps 139). We have been graced with the Divine Image in our human soul. We have by the resurrection of the Lord Jesus Christ died with Christ and have risen with him (Rom 6:4).

Scripture reminds us that we are not just flesh and blood. We were given a soul, a spirit who lives within us that cries out "Abba" (Rom 8:15). It is our spiritual body, undernourished by our own lack of prayer and intimacy with God, which is languishing, crying out to be healed. Truth be told, we eat physically twenty-one times in a seven-day week, at a minimum, but we feed our spiritual bodies only one hour (if we make it to Mass) a week. Then, we cannot understand why our prayers seem unanswered, or why God's absence is so often present. We are so spiritually malnourished that we even forget the reality that God desires we be healed.

The Gospels are emphatic in teaching us that Jesus is entirely concerned with the spiritual well being of those he encounters. He is rarely concerned with the physical healing of people, but he is always concerned with their spiritual healing. He is never ashamed to tell the afflicted that their sins are forgiven (Mark 2:1–12). It is only to challenge the disbelief of the hard-hearted that Jesus adds to the spiritual healing the human concern and desire of physical healing (Mark 2:10–12).

The Gospel story of the healing of a paralyzed man is a classic example of Jesus' attitude towards the healing of an individual (Mark 2:1–12). The story portrays Jesus as truly being focused on the spiritual paralysis of the man rather than on any type of immediate concern or preoccupation with his ability to walk. Jesus is more concerned with the paralyzed man's finding forgiveness for his sins rather than whether or not he can pick up his mat and walk. Where everyone desires to see the physical reconstruction of sinews, bone, and muscle, Jesus desires that the man be freed from the spiritual paralysis which has not let him walk free. Jesus' concern is that the soul of the man be able to soar once again.

Imagine the paralyzed man. Imagine his incredulity of being lifted and hoisted by his friends with all of the bystanders hollering and shoving. Imagine the fears of the paralyzed man as he is lowered before the Lord. All through his paralyzed life he has had to make different provisions for himself. All of his paralyzed life, he has had to live with the stigma of somehow having been cursed by life and God. All of his paralyzed life he has had to confront family and friends as less than normal. All of his paralyzed life he has prayed to God the Almighty that he walk again. How did he feel when after all of the efforts of his friends and after all his prayers and hopes he heard the Miracle Worker tell him that his sins were forgiven?

Imagine the four friends of the paralyzed man. Their actions and hopes were placed in the reputation of Jesus the Miracle Worker touching and healing their friend. Imagine the incredible and tremendous faith of those men who lowered the paralyzed man in front of the Lord Jesus.

With faith and hope, they went beyond the ordinary seeking the extraordinary. They went beyond their anticipation of expecting Jesus to heal their friend physically. How did they feel when they heard that Jesus was saying that the sins of their friend were forgiven?

Imagine the crowded house where the Lord was teaching. Imagine all of the people stuffed into the room trying to hear the words of the Teacher. Imagine the scribes and Pharisees engaging the Lord in debate over the Torah and its implications as they tried not to touch the unclean who were listening just as attentively. Imagine the noise and smells which filled the room, when suddenly the roof above their heads begins to be removed. The crowded room forces people to stand shoulder to shoulder with their backs to the wall. The makeshift pulley coming from the ceiling scattered the crowd so that they not be hit by the object descending from above them. Imagine the gasps and the shouting. Imagine the never-ending quest to maintain ritual purity as people are shoved against each other.

Then as everyone's gaze follows the mat from the ceiling to the feet of the Lord, the people hear the words of the Lord. They are waiting to see a miracle of miracles. The scribes and Pharisees await the show. The poor and marginalized await an act of compassion. The four friends await the miracle. The paralyzed man awaits his future.

Then the Lord speaks. The Word of God proclaims forgiveness. The incredible drama illustrating the Lord's concern for spiritual wholeness takes place. Jesus tells the paralyzed man that his sins are forgiven. The words flow naturally from his lips without any qualms. The words are spoken as if there were never any doubt that these were the most correct words to be spoken (Isa 55:10–11). What were they expecting him to say? The blessing is bestowed on the paralytic as simply as saying, "Let there be light" (Gen 1:3).

The gasps can be heard all the way to the crowd gathered outside the house. The blessing of forgiveness seems impossible to everyone. The blessing of forgiveness is unthinkable. What is on everyone's mind is the physical healing of the paralysis. It is unimaginable that forgiveness would even be mentioned, especially when it is so obvious that the man desires to walk. Forgiveness belongs to the Divine.

No one can forgive sins but God. Everyone in the crowded room knows that fact, even those ignorant of the Torah. Even the poor have been taught that only God can forgive a person his sins. Even the unclean know that God alone forgives sins. Where did Jesus ever fathom that he could even pronounce the blessing of forgiveness? How is it possible that after all of the teaching and debate which had been going on previously has now manifested itself in the unthinkable, the highly controversial blessing of forgiveness?

An interesting moment occurs after the blessing of forgiveness. It is a time of human embarrassment based in self-righteousness. Everyone in the room and outside the house is thinking the same thing. The studious and the ignorant, the rich and the poor, the healthy and the infirm, the ritually clean and impure are all pondering the words they just heard. It is unbelievable, yet no one dares to mention to the Teacher his error, his blasphemy.

Jesus unabashedly knows their doubts and wonderment. He too is embarrassed by their lack of understanding, their human need for physical proof of the love of God. Rather than let them live in ignorance and ready to challenge their faith with one more engaging didactic, he asks them as to which is easier to say: that the sins of the paralytic are forgiven or that the man stand up, pick up his mat, and walk. Which is easier to say: that the spiritual paralysis of the man is over and healed or that the physical body is healed only to suffer death at a later date?

Jesus, ever desiring spiritual healing yet knowing the unbelief of his people, provides the physical proof for them in order that they may know that the Son of Man has authority on earth to forgive sins. Jesus is emphatic that his mission is based on the desire that the people of God be a forgiven people who return to the Lord God. His mission was never one to heal only the physical body. The Son of Man, the Word of God, holding the power of forgiveness which breaks all spiritual paralysis, heals the physical infirmity so that the people will understand that forgiveness of sins is far more important than the ability to walk. The miracle is not the physical healing of the paralytic. The miracle is that forgiveness of sins heals the soul.

There is no court of creation. There is no celestial court which rules over humanity. It is the love of God which has the final say in our lives. Scripture reminds us that God so loved the world (John 3:16). God's love decides the measure of how this world will be judged. The Scriptures teach us that God did not send his Son into the world to condemn it but that it might be saved through him. (John 3:17). St. Paul is emphatic in his stance that because we belong to Christ, there exists nothing in this created world or in the celestial which has the power to separate us from the love of God which we have experienced in Christ Jesus (Rom 8:31-39). However evocative the moon and stars may be of our feelings in the blur of loving and hate-filled moments, creation operates impervious to or ignorant of human feelings.

The devastated spouse, spiritually paralyzed, sought some type of maladjusted vengeance. The obsession would not let the spouse walk. There was no way to get to the Lord because the all-consuming hurt had even damaged her trust level with God. We always have access to God and his justice. There are no appellate court levels which speak on behalf of the Lord. The Lord's justice has no courts and cases. The justice of God is that his Son died on a cross so that we might be saved. The love of God for us is inexhaustible. As no parent desires to see a child suffer, then even less so does the Lord God desire to see us hurt (Luke 11:11–13). He desires even less that we hurt ourselves.

Courts of creation and celestial beings born of hurt and depression and filtered through alcohol and self-destructive measures are the antithesis of the Paschal Mystery. The wife desired pain for the "ex", not justice. She sought misery and vengeance for the dysfunctional lover. Alcohol and depression paralyzed the grieving "ex." It was impossible to get to the Lord not only because of the spiritual paralysis of the devastated spouse but also because her house was crowded with hurtful memories of right and wrong. It was filled with words of "I said, you said." The house overflowed with unexpressed feelings shoving each other around the mental abode and still trying to maintain a ritual purity of no culpability in the separation and divorce.

When the "ex" received ass warts, it was not the judgment of any court of creation. It was not the will of God responding to the desire of a hurting vengeful spouse that an "ex" suffer. If God could be manipulated into vengeful hurt or fulfilling hateful desires, the world would have ceased to exist centuries ago. Ass warts were the consequences of human sexual activity. The curses and condemnations of the inconsolable spouse were the human consequences of human rage and obsession. Which is easier to say: your hate and obsession are forgiven or burn off the warts?

The only way for the devastated spouse to begin the process of regaining wholeness once again is to allow friends to carry her back to the Lord. Let the friends open the roof of crowded painful memories so that she may be lowered to the feet of the Lord. Let the grieving one be lowered to the feet of God within a room redolent of seventeen years and 331 days of good times and bad, richness and poverty, sickness and health; all the marriage memories will see what the Teacher will do.

The only way to physical healing is to understand that the Lord has forgiven the spouse her sins. It is the soul of the devastated one which the Lord desires to heal. It is the Divine Image in the aggrieved that the Lord seeks to uncover that he might see once again the beauty of what he created and not the mire of what she has made of life. When the devastated spouse, paralyzed in spirit and soul, accepts the gentle forgiveness uttered with the same intensity as a new creation, then and only then will she be able to stand up, pick up her life, and walk again.

The ex-husband, too, needs healing. Although he is unable to discern it now, he too is spiritually paralyzed, unable to see his incapacity to address his feelings honestly with himself and with his "ex." His self-absorption, like the anger of the devastated one, consumes him. Since he cannot see how his actions and feelings affect others, he lives in his own fantasy world where he has done no wrong and people whom he has hurt are of no real consequence. At the most, his behavior is solipsistic; at the least, it is masturbatory. His self-absorption manifests itself in non-communication and distancing so as not to incite feelings of guilt and loss within himself, but always with the unstated goal of not having to face the hurt he has caused other people in his life and love life as well.

His inability to recognize the hurt he has caused for many years, and not only in the separation and divorce, paralyzes his own relationships. People whom he has known have become disposable when they outlive their usefulness to him. His pattern of behavior is strewn with dead relationships, male and female. Dishonest he lives behind a façade. He has convinced himself that he is honorable. His actions suggest the idea that other people are for his use or pleasure. His commitment to relationships ceases, and even professed marriage vows are worthless as soon as they no longer serve his interests. Even God is at his disposal. Incapable of empathy and blind to any culpability or participation on his part, he is his own truth.

The Lord desires that both be healed. Healing will occur, however, only when there is recognition of moral paralysis. The paralyzed man of the Gospel must have cried in joy and wonder when he heard the Lord speak to him of forgiveness. Perhaps he was the only one in the room for whom this blessing was enough. Hearing the words Jesus pronounced to the depths of his soul that has been wholly forgiven eliminates any and all desire for any physical miracle. Not only did he walk physically, he walked forgiven, in the profound understanding that God loved him. He walked knowing now in front of all the people that God had always loved him and that nothing could ever paralyze or impede that grace.

Divorce paralyzes people. It does not let them walk free. Friends are all around trying to lower us to the feet of the Lord. It is their faith that has the power to confront the depressive sadness paralyzing the divorced. It is the Lord's desire to pronounce the blessing of forgiveness that we might walk again in grace and wholeness. Every divorced person must confront the moments of spiritual paralysis affecting their lives. Divorced persons must discern the four friends who truly come to them with the gift of faith desiring the healing from the Lord. They must trust beyond all trust. Ultimately, divorced persons must struggle in faith to allow the process of recovery to occur if they ever desire to walk again, but to walk again forgiven: *the deep heartfelt understanding of being loved by God.*

A PRAYER FOR HEALING

I cannot see Lord.
I am unable to walk.
Life has numbed all my senses.

I cannot see you, Lord.
I am unable to walk to you.
Life has numbed my trust in you, Lord.

I see painful memories.
I walk stumbling all the way.
I am numb to all creation around me.

Touch me gently.
Whisper softly once again.
Caress my soul.
I know you are there.

7

The Smallest Dick in the World

DIVORCE TERMINATES A RELATIONSHIP which terminated long ago. Divorce is the legal and final act of stating the relationship is dead. Even though divorce publicly states the relationship is over, the consequences of the broken relationship persist. They manifest themselves in consuming anger and barbed retorts. Feelings take precedence over any court decision. Feelings of bitterness can become so intense, so consuming, that in order for life to move beyond the bitterness of anger and hate, the simple daily routines must go on. They must continue, however, with a redefining of the person, a redefinition of discovering once again who the person is whom God created. The goal for any divorced person is to move beyond anger to forgiving oneself without seeking vengeance.

What has been lost? Why does one need to forgive oneself? Like an onion peeled and finding nothing in the center, a divorce reeks with a haunting smell throughout the room producing tears as involuntary as in cutting an onion. As they unravel their history, ex-spouses often exude an unbearable smell as past memories, good and bad alike, fill their lives only to find that, like the onion, their lives have nothing that held them together in the first place. Both are as empty on the inside of the relationship as the divorce announces publicly to the outside.

Laden with emptiness, the relationship has cried for an outlet for some time until finally the inevitable had to happen. As necessary as that it had to happen, separation and divorce leave a residue of broken dreams, broken promises, and a public and private display of emotional hurt. It is inevitable that the divorced grieve over the loss of their relationship. It is, however, sometimes a grieving which necessitates a premise. As the feelings become so intense and the tears so constant, or as depression sometimes becomes the norm, even the grieving cries out for a redefinition.

Feelings that accompany the sense of loss cry out as well for some type of purification. The actual grieving needs to be redirected in order that the divorced may truly appreciate exactly what has been lost. Relationships, even those which break, do not and cannot live in perennial hate and tension. As the vows state, "in good times and bad," every relationship moves through stages of happiness and sadness. Relationships that end in separation and divorce tend to focus solely on the bad times. The grief is sometimes so profound as to erase memories of good times. Although they may be miniscule, the good times, too, affect the grieving process.

Grieving implies that love had a part in the relationship. We cry only for those persons whom we have loved. Our tears are reserved for the persons and moments which actually meant something to us. We do not mourn over something or someone who has not touched us in some manner at some deeper level of our lives. The very act of crying suggests that lives are rendered different because of the interaction with that someone for whom we cared.

Even in the most abusive and bitter of relationships there was at one time a moment of love and caring. No matter how the relationship may have deteriorated, two people who hate each other cannot bind themselves together. At a very different and maybe deeply hidden level, the couple at one time did share feelings for one another. In memories of long ago and once upon a time, they were probably defined as feelings of love, and they were mutual feelings.

Those shared feelings, mistakenly called "love," throughout the separation and divorce most assuredly take a beating. As the reality of single life begins to take root in the divorced, those shared feelings living in memory, now cluttered and dominated by the bad times, still try to ingratiate themselves into part of the lived history. They are in all actuality probably the source of many tears. Many believe that the tears which are shed come from the rupture and anger one has experienced in the separation and divorce process. To a large extent, this is true. Raw feelings do produce tears.

There is, however, another side to those tears, not just hate that evokes such strong emotion. The original shared feelings of love also contribute to the intense emotional outbreaks. Shared moments of good times also call forth the tenderness of tears. Those good times, rattled and shaken, beaten and tortured by the process of divorce may seem defunct, but in reality they are last gasps of life which tenderize the grieving moments.

Seemingly lifeless, the once shared feelings of good times still evoke tears at what has been lost.

What has been lost? Grieving is rooted in the realization that the long ago good times never blossomed. The bad times dominate the history and memory; they overshadow the reality that the relationship did begin quite differently. Shared good times are not dead. They are like seeds which never flowered, yet everyone knows they were planted. They are still there in the soil of the relationship. It is just that the weeds of bad times have choked the growth (Matt 13:7).

Sometimes the intense hurt of the divorce makes it more difficult to remember the good times which did occur. The hurt of being broken tends to overwhelm the emotional state of the divorced so that they cannot see or even less remember how or when good times ceased to exist. The loss of memory about the good times does not mean that they did not occur. The pain of divorce has simply blurred the memory until it makes a conscious decision to prefer loss to remembering. New patterns emerge as signs of trouble leading to the inevitability of divorce. Sometimes that same pain causes a divorced person to remember, but always from the unhealthy viewpoint of anger based on disappointment.

Whether or not there is a conscious decision not to remember or to remember from an angry perspective, the shared good times become the framework for the grief and loss. It is an irony of life that it is actually the shared good times which shape and form the process of grief. Shared good times seem to revel in the midst of pain and anger. When all of the focus is on the wrongs which occurred in the marriage, separation, and even the divorce, the shared good times give the grieving process its identity. We cry only for that which we have loved. Our tears are shed when we lose what we treasured in this life.

What has been lost? Grieving is most intense when spouses realize that what has been lost is friendship. Out of all the anger and arguments, the belittling and berating, the cursing and castigating, the original friendship has been strained and beaten. Friendship has been lost.

As friends, the couple shared everything. They shared the most intimate of details and found strength from one another in their sharing. Sexual lovemaking sprang from the friendship. Divorce has fractured the friendship of the couple. The one person upon whom the other relied has been taken out of the equation and has become the one person with whom neither will share anything anymore, except in the cases of children.

Personal successes and failures, hopes and dreams, fears and tears are now dealt with individually. They may be shared with family, friends, and even casual acquaintances, but the one person whose approval resounded throughout the relationship of marriage is gone and may care less about the personal life of the ex-spouse. It is a myth, a lie that the divorced often tell themselves that their "ex" is actually thinking about them. The "ex" does not worry or care about the wellbeing of the one left behind. The hurtful reality is that the "ex" never thought often enough about the spouse during the marriage. Why would an "ex" now become a considerate compassionate human being if in the marriage, concern for the other was rarely an issue?

The friendship is gone. It is over. It becomes evident then that many tears and much worry arise from the loss of friendship. It is disturbing to think that one has shared so much with another person on the most intimate of levels, naked and knowing no shame (Gen 2:25), only to learn later that the other hasn't an inkling of desire to maintain the friendship.

Loss of friendship renders the entire relationship meaningless. It causes one to doubt if there were ever any friendship which mattered much or at all. Loss of friendship plants seeds of doubt and frustration. Doubt and frustration sprinkled with the recent memories of bad times are causes for the tears arising from the divorce. Tears make one speculate about the actual sincerity of the friendship from its very inception.

Who cares how many love letters were exchanged if in the end they amounted to nothing? Who cares if cards and flowers were given if in the end the cards were a waste of trees and the flowers went the way of all flesh? Who cares how many times one was told that he or she was loved when in all reality the other partner might not even spell the word much less understand what it truly meant? Who cares how many intimate relational aspects of life were shared if at the root lay a lie?

The sharing of life and intimate details of the soul which formed the friendship resulted in a marriage covenant. Loss of the framework of friendship blurs the good memories with the more powerful difficult ones and allows the bad times to overwhelm the good. Blurred and mixed memories, like water and sand, erase hints of the purity and wholeness of the friendship.

The tears, coming forth as an outgrowth of the blurring, express grief over the loss of friendship and the inability to distinguish good memories from difficult ones. Without any sense of vision, everything seems bad except that the soul knows of good times as well. It is simply impossible to recapture the memories of good times when the memories are swirling around in a mud puddle of anger. The result is a disastrous flood of tears not knowing whence they come when everything points to the bleakness of the relationship and a future alone.

Friends and family are many times less supportive than they perceive themselves to be. They want the divorced person to move on with life and cannot understand where the tears are coming from if the relationship needed ending in the first place. They cannot possibly understand or grasp why the divorcing partners waste so much time worrying about what is past and over, especially when it has become so evident that the relationship was over long before any actual acknowledgment of its death. Friends and family somehow miss the point that the couple at one time were friends, and the friendship is dead.

Anger always manifests itself in some manner or another. Grief does the same thing, for it cannot be suppressed forever. Even if it is only the soul of the divorced that knows the reason for its grief, it will be the soul crying very human tears. Like anger, grief can manifest itself in very positive and negative ways with little attention to whom or what may be in its path. Grief simply has to be expressed.

With the death of friendship, the soul must grieve. Through memories the soul recalls moments of kindness and wonders what occurred to destroy them. The soul will doubt why the good times could not be restored or even maintained. It will always mourn what once was living in wonder and why it is not to be repeated anymore. The soul, when every other aspect of life seems to have gone beyond the separation and divorce, will cry very human tears as it meditates and blames, as it reflects and seeks understandable answers. It is much easier to raise Lazarus from the dead than to resurrect a friendship killed in divorce (John 11).

With all of the memories which accompany any grief process and with all of the times which pray for just one more episode of "if I only had one more chance," grief roots itself in a critical blaming moment which simply rubs the sore rawer. Blaming is the ever-familiar game in which one tries to justify an action at the expense of some other cause.

Naturally the blame begins with all of the peccadilloes of the ex-spouse. Blame conjures up old sayings and looks for odd moments which may be clues to the inevitable separation. Blaming, as it begins the process of character assassination of the ex-spouse, eventually takes its toll on the one citing the violations of the failed matrimonial vows. Looking and searching for more fodder, the blaming process eventually turns in on the blamer. Blaming the ex-spouse leads one right to the moment of blaming oneself.

In the divorce process the blaming of self is the most delicate. Self-hate emerging from self-blaming brings grief loaded with anger which cries from the innermost depths of the self for peace. From the reality of knowing what has been lost, the friendship, springs forth the next level in the healing process, the concept of forgiveness.

Why does one have to forgive oneself? This is the most difficult question to answer in that it is linked to the memory of the sins and actions of the ex-spouse. The initial blaming centered on the wrong and hurtful actions of the "ex" with little to no attention that a marriage is comprised of two individuals. If two make a marriage, then all of the actions of that marriage invariably involve both persons.

This concept, the forgiveness of oneself, is the most difficult for the hurting ex-spouse to see or understand. Since the days of the separation and divorce, one has focused so hard and diligently on the wrongs of the other, that it has become much more difficult to realize one's own culpability in the break-up of the marriage. The very thought that one might need to forgive oneself is incomprehensible no matter how much one's soul hurts.

Forgiveness of self, however, is the only way out of the depression and sadness emanating from the loss of friendship. The loss of friendship can be so traumatic that it requires forgiveness of oneself. Forgiveness of oneself is an honest acknowledgment of one's own culpability in the break-up and subsequent loss of the marriage. It acknowledges to one's own soul that grief over the loss of friendship has origins in behavior. The consequence of the tears comes from a relationship of two not one. Forgiveness of self admits the truth that "I too have wronged an individual whom I loved." Forgiveness of self admits that the vows taken were not taken seriously or attended to equally by both parties.

As soon as forgiveness of self begins, the blaming becomes less intense. The blaming of the other spouse or of oneself diminishes in intensity as reason starts reorganizing life to a healthier equanimity. Forgiveness of self acknowledges the weaknesses of both individuals in the marital relationship and highlights the crucial areas which simply could not be maintained (communication, recreation, trust, mutuality).

Forgiveness of self involves an honest examination of conscience from the hurting individual. It asks the individual to put aside the blatant blunders of the ex-spouse and to concentrate on one's own actions and behaviors. Forgiveness of self does not concentrate on blaming. It forces the individual to look at the whole of life in order that life may be made whole again. Forgiveness of self asks the individual to look at life from before the marriage relationship began. It asks for a personal inventory of one's whole life up to the point when the vows were exchanged.

Forgiveness of self attempts to identify the patterns of one's behavior, highlighting trends in relationships with all people and not just the particular relationship with the spouse. Forgiveness of self is not an easy task because without any assignation of blame, it asks the individual to be honest with himself or herself in looking at past relationships from the familial to the personal to see where mistakes may have occurred.

Forgiveness of self points out in its own tenderness where lack of communication may have occurred before ever meeting the spouse. It does not hide the moment(s) where lack of trust was bred into the life fabric of the individual. Forgiveness of self is acute in pointing out the importance of recreation (being re-created) in all relationships. It admits to the joy that ought to be in one's life and the devastating consequence when joy is forgotten to the point of erasure. Forgiveness of self acknowledges that humanity was created in partnership and friendship abhorring the tendency to isolation, greed, and shame (Gn 3:8-10).

The difficulty inherent in the process of forgiving oneself is that it requires an individual to go beyond the present grief over the loss of friendship and to see a broader and wider picture of one's life. Forgiveness of self asks to do the difficult task of personal inventory of unhealed wounds, still lingering and festering in the soul. Those unhealed wounds of life before the marriage covenant produce an abominable stench stinking the temple of the Lord with an odor of rotting creaturely flesh rather than the fragrant offering one's life should be.

It is difficult to concentrate on the life before marriage because when the couple entered into marriage they actually believed they were capable of living those vows as no other couple had before them. The couple never reviewed the impact that their own unhealed wounds would have upon their new relationship with someone who was promising to love them beyond all imagining. Forgiveness of self looks to the life of the individual before he or she ever decided to enter into this committed relationship.

The process is difficult because we do not recognize how often our own unhealed, unexamined wounds of the past affect our patterns of behavior now in the present. The loss of friendships from our earlier years, the times of sharing and being betrayed by so-called friends, the fights in home or school, the discovery of one's self in its acceptance and rejection by others—all contribute to the make-up of our personality and the patterns of our behavioral interaction with others.

Forgiveness of self does not have any dealings with "I lied, I cheated, I stole." Forgiveness of self zeroes in on the multiple moments of one's humanity when "I felt, I hurt, I cried." Forgiveness of self looks into and highlights those moments when for very different reasons one's relationships were broken and confused, when the rupture of honesty took place at one's expense.

Forgiveness of self understands that past moments of hurt may have never been healed. They have, on the other hand, acted as major influences in one's life. Never tended to, they often have been controlling factors in one's life. They should have been put to rest long ago. Forgiveness of self does not look to blame. It does not look to assign any culpability to parents or family, culture or conditions. If in retrospective self-examination, blaming begins to occur, it is not forgiveness of self. It is simply blaming, looking for some type of self-justification to absolve the false self.

Forgiveness of self does not have at its interest any motive to assign blame. It looks to see how untreated wounds of the past have influenced patterns of behavior. It illumines our past sores that we might heal. An intense examination of one's life will show how wounds of the past affect our speech, our thoughts, our concepts, our aspirations and dreams, our failures and errors.

Before ever reaching the broad waters of separation and divorce, there is a vast ocean of past unhealed wounds crying for attention and balm. Forgiveness of self arising from the soul's grief in the loss of friendship goes one giant step beyond the disastrous feelings of divorce to minister to the roots of hurt. Forgiveness of self looks to healing by God's grace a whole life not just one obvious hurt like divorce.

The process of forgiving oneself, as necessary as it may be, is not an easy task. It involves a deep honesty in order that he or she can delve into a past to see which memories still evoke feelings of angst. It looks to uncover once again those moments of frustration and tears which painted the world in different shades of blue and never received an appropriate answer as to why that color.

In order that the forgiveness of self be concentrated on a broader vision of self, the person must acknowledge the obvious. Journal writing is the best approach whether it be in a personal diary format or sitting at the computer. Either way the intention is the same: thoughts and memories of past hurts be put in writing.

A personal note should be written stating that these are the people or moments in my life which have not been healed. Those people or moments which damaged me should be listed like a grocery list. Do not be afraid to tell yourself the truth. Do not blame but recognize first how the past has affected your present and then realize how far the Lord has brought you.

In a journal write the title: "People who have hurt me." Number the incidents or people in a list. Start with numbers one to twenty-five. Put the name of the ex-spouse as number one with a colon stating my divorce. This is the unhealed wound which consistently cries for forgiveness of self. Then begin with number two. Begin thinking of your growing-up years. What were the moments which disturbed you in those elementary years? Who was the person with whom you fought at home, school, or the playground? Whose interaction caused stress in your life? Number these people and events as you would a roll call and begin the process.

In the quiet of reflection begin with number two. Do not start with your divorce. It is not helpful at this juncture. Starting with the ex-spouse will illicit only anger and blame and will eventually frustrate the process of forgiving oneself.

Beginning with number two, start to recall how you were hurt by the second person or event. Why does it still stay in your memory? What is it that bothers you about the manner in which this incident was dealt with or not dealt with at that time? How would you deal with it now knowing what you know? What mistake occurred with this person or incident? Did you try to win a friendship? Did you play up to someone pretending to be what you are not? Did any arrogance enter into the situation? Did you impose your own values blinding any honest understanding or mutual communication?

Continue this same process with everyone you must list. You will find that some people will require great thought while others come easily. The most important aspect of this exercise is to write the feelings of the moment, how you dealt with the incident, and how you would deal with it now. Discover what it is about the incident that made you hurt. Understand how that moment or person influenced you by the hurt that occurred. Realize how you have moved beyond that hurt. If you have not, then it becomes even more incumbent to acknowledge its controlling influence in your life in order that you might regain control of your life.

This process should be continued with everyone and every event you list. You will find that listing and writing past names and events evoke other memories so that the list might grow even though you believed that you had moved beyond those hurtful moments of life. Never attempt to write about your number-one unhealed wound—the divorce—because it will distract you from the forgiveness process designed for you. It is a better practice to start with number two concentrating on only one number at each sitting. Do not try to list and write everything in one sitting. Allow yourself the peace of mind that each incident is worthy of the Lord's forgiveness as if a thousand years were as a day.

At each sitting write the name of the person and state what is the unhealed wound crying for balm. Begin to describe in as much detail as possible the memory of the event. Write all of the feelings you felt when it occurred. Try to discover the why of the miscommunication and mistrust of the event. Attempt to uncover negative feelings. Look at the wound still unhealed and determine what it will take for it to begin to be treated.

This exercise of the memory should be repeated with everyone who has been mentioned on the list. The process should be given adequate time and patience so that you may allow the self to be forgiven of the past. This process allows forgiveness to replace blame of self or others. It attempts to teach that we are who we are because we have been formed over a lifetime.

Too many times we attempt to deny the bad and difficult times in our life believing the myth or the lie that to forget is to forgive. It is better to remember and move forward than to deny the parts of our life that have formed and molded us. Remembering past events and seeking their healing will expose the roots of what occurred in the marital relationship. It is a grave mistake to try to erase difficult past events because from past wounds a person has become the person he or she is now.

Eventually the process must be done for the number-one person, the ex-spouse, listed on the list, but avoid the temptation to begin there. It is better to look at the forgiveness of self through the eyes of past events before the marriage covenant was even an idea. Citing and realizing that one entered into the marriage relationship as an already broken individual and linked up with another broken individual makes more sense as to why the problems occurred in the marriage and led to the subsequent separation and divorce.

Forgiveness of self demands a tremendous amount of honesty in order that the self may be freed from the guilt which attaches itself so frequently to spirituality. Our relationship with God does not expose guilt; it seeks honest relationship. If forgiveness of self is to be achieved, the process of looking at unhealed wounds has to occur. That process will open up the self to many painful memories which have often continued to influence one's current behavior. Looking at past unhealed wounds, however, is only a part of the healing process of self.

The process must also be done for the wounds which one has caused in another's life. In order for a person to have the grace to forgive himself, he must also consider and prayerfully look at the people in his life whom he has hurt. This is a difficult part of the process of forgiving oneself because it demands that a person admit to being the cause of pain to another person.

The process should be written out as precisely as in the process for looking at people who have been the cause of unhealed wounds in one's life. A different journal should carry this process. Begin in the same manner. Write a short note stating that these are the people to whom I have been a cause of pain. Make a list. The number-one person should be the name of the ex-spouse. Then in the same manner, list people in your early childhood for whom you were the cause of pain for any reason. As the list continues to grow, apply the same process to this new list.

Do not begin with number one, the ex-spouse. Begin with number two stating how you caused pain in another's life. What were the circumstances which caused the rupture? What were the feelings that were expressed or unspoken? What was the result? What was the hurt you hurled and why did it occur?

This process of looking at people whom I have hurt is extremely important in that it broadens one's vision to see how a reciprocal process of interaction affects all of our life. Many times the events and moments we disliked in our life were also the events and moments of pain that we caused in the life of another. We know that fact mentally, but it consistently eludes us when we are hurting. We forget that somehow we too were the cause of pain in someone else's life.

Forgiveness of self can truly be realized if we allow ourselves to be open to looking honestly at those two major areas of our life before we ever look at the hurt of divorce:

A. examining those who have hurt me and left unhealed wounds in my life, and

B. examining those whom I have hurt and left unhealed wounds in their lives.

Both exercises should be done without ever referring to the ex-spouse. There are so many issues which should be covered before the marriage rupture should be addressed. The honesty needed to look at both sides of the hurt issue is one which requires the patience of tears in order that the soul may truly resonate in peace. This journaling can be very time consuming, but the naming and writing of the past gives light and clarity to the present.

Journaling about both issues of hurt (received and given) before ever reaching the marriage and divorce issues allows the self to be bathed in the knowledge that God has continued to love all in all. Journaling and naming reminds us that the love of God has never ceased. It is that tender love which still caresses the person to be healed of the pain of divorce.

Both issues, naming those who have hurt me and those whom I have hurt, are difficult. Both will come full circle to embrace the divorce issue with the same tenderness as looking at one's own soul. Journaling in honesty, examining the past with the intent of forgiving oneself, will remove one from the blame game. It will give a true inner peace to replace the hatred which always accompanies any blame whether it be of the ex-spouse or of oneself. Forgiveness of self, embracing both sides of the hurting issue, has absolutely no concept of blame. The end result, therefore, can only be the healing of the soul in order that life may be lived in abundance once again.

CASE STUDY

The couple went through a seemingly peaceful separation and divorce. It was a quick process but left many of the issues still buried without honest communication. The marriage had been lived in good times and bad. It could speak of its richness and poverty and had gone beyond the sickness and health of the couple. It just could not last until death parted them. Communication had broken down immensely. Fidelity had never been a strong component of either spouse. Neither one, however, spoke of their infidelities to the other. Extra-marital affairs were an ongoing activity, but it was never mentioned.

One of the spouses had a long affair with another during the marriage. He never questioned his infidelity. He believed in his heart that everything was fine so long as his spouse never knew of it. It was not adultery, he imagined, if the spouse did not know it was occurring. It became an adulterous affair only if he were caught. Naturally this granted him the mental license to have sex at his pleasure, just discreetly.

He believed his marriage was healthy and saw no problem in having his special affair. After all, he had had other affairs but had enough sense never to mention them. His concept of fidelity was that he was married, and this was the only person who meant everything to him. His extra-marital affairs were just that, extra-marital. It was of no consideration to him that his infidelity had also occurred while he was in the dating period.

Throughout the marriage he had different other lovers but never viewed those relationships as interfering with his marriage. Even towards the end of the marriage he maintained one special affair and mentally justified that nothing was wrong with it. Once the divorce was final, he maintained his affair. One of his problems is that he never viewed the extra relationship as anything but normal. No one knew of it, though some suspected. The privacy of the affair was not just crucial; it was mandatory since the other person in the affair was a newlywed. The affair was with a married person—double adultery.

This relationship had been going on for some years. The wedding of the newlywed meant nothing to either of the participants when they were having sexual relations. They both lived with the same philosophy: so long as their spouse was ignorant of the extra-marital affair, then it was not an affair. The man practiced strictly an old Mexican adage: where there is no gentleman, there is no lady, that is, not naming your affairs presumes respectability.

When the older man went through his divorce, it was not even mentioned as he and his lover engaged in sexual romps. This morally twisted relationship continued for at least seven years of the man's marriage and at least two years into the beginning of the separation and divorce years. It would have continued even longer if the newlywed had not moved to another city.

Because the affair was a normal part of the man's life, he never saw it as something which would determine his life. There was no future in the relationship. It was simply sexual, and because it was so natural and exclusive, it did not factor into the man's urge to heal beyond the divorce. He maintained grief at the loss of his marriage but never saw the affair as being a factor in the disintegration of the marriage.

Daily he cursed his broken marriage and his ex-spouse. Alcohol played a large part in his grieving. His healing was taking a normal path, but it laid heavily on his heart that in this world, he was alone. He had to date again. Dating became a huge fear in rebuilding his life. He had to engage himself in relationship once again.

After so many years of marriage, his identity was very tied to his spouse. He had to define himself once again. It was a horrible healing process. He suffered from major depression and soothed his feelings with alcohol. His obsession with the divorce in his life led him to the point of a nervous breakdown. Although the sexual activity continued with the other partner, it never entered into his mind that he was still in a relationship. All he could fathom was that he was no longer married to the person whom he loved. It never dawned on him that his affairs destroyed his marriage.

The year after the divorce was disastrous. He continued his special affair but never saw that as anything unusual. His fears about re-building his life were overwhelming. He maintained a prestigious work position and hid his grief as best he could. His close friends shied away from the topic because of the man's obsession with the grief. Erroneously, the man believed he could express his feelings to his friends. They were not interested or perhaps could not bear the intensity of his hurt. Once he confessed to a close friend his thoughts of suicide. The friend gave the familiar comfort in stressful times but never broached the subject again. The friend never asked or inquired about the mental health of the man. It was just too frightening a responsibility.

The man was a professional and tried his best not to let his grief affect his position. He was most successful in suppressing his grief in public, but it did manifest itself in inappropriate manners at times. He could become sore with employees for little reason. Aware of his proclivity to explode and rather than take it out on minor incompetents, vendors usually received the brunt of the suppressed grieving. The obsession with his work in order to go beyond his grief produced over three-million dollars gain in his business, but it could not soothe the bleeding wound of his broken marriage.

He could motivate large groups of people in their jobs, yet his personal life was totally unmanageable. People who thought they knew him would never have conceived that he lived in a brokenness that filled his personal life. Because of his position and managerial skills, he knew many people, but very few people actually knew him. Considering the state of his emotions, he was a disaster, but on the outside, he was a master of a good and cheerful appearance.

He dwelt on his losses and could not see the success he had achieved. The one for whom he had lived for many years had left him. The part of his life which had strengthened him had been removed. His other half, the other side of his personality, was no longer. He walked and moved in the darkness of grief. He did not even know who he was without his spouse. He tried to remember his life before the ex-spouse, but found it impossible to recover. He was no longer that person.

Being a professional man, he knew he needed professional help. He went to some counseling sessions and began a painful rebuilding process. The counselor never knew of the special affair which was still going on. Appropriately, the man began with the process of re-defining his life without the ex-spouse. Who was he? Who was he without that other person? He used to watch two situation comedies, a practice that became just as obsessive as his grief over the divorce. He would tape the television shows so that late at night he could enter into a different world of comedy allowing the shows to teach him again the inanity of being a human being in relationships.

The comedies, *Third Rock From The Sun* and *Will and Grace,* provided the laughs at life the man needed. They illustrated to him that relationship has no definite boundaries except to be honest with oneself. His journaling riddled with past pains, depicted a man living in the grief moment of happy-to-be-out-of-the-marriage yet devastated by the immense loss in his life. The television comedies, taped, watched, and re-watched, put laughter back in the man's life. He identified with the slap-stick, the messiness of relationships, the folly of being human. These comedies with their focus on all the human frailties of life became in a very strange way the needed balm he was looking for to soothe his hurts. They reminded him that humanity finds its blessing in its imperfections.

In inexplicable ways, the television situation comedies helped him put life back into an order he could understand. It was, perhaps, the inanity of looking at one's own follies which helped him to realize the imperfection of his past actions. He knew he had to move beyond. The difficulty lay in the impossible dream to which he clung that one day he and his ex-spouse would be together again. The difficulties with television sit-coms is that they are two dimensional, and he was a living a three-dimensional divorced life. There were no laugh tracks to put crisis moments at ease. The sit-coms did not show the reality of alcoholism and grief. His grief was not a timed seven-minute exposé of his life with commercials in between in order to get through the plot of his life by the end of a half-hour. There were no commercial breaks for his tears.

It was a strange time in his life. The prospect of going on a date terrified him immensely. His other affair surprisingly did not provide him any confidence in this personal matter. As he felt himself growing in self-confidence, he looked to an upcoming professional conference he was to attend. He prepared himself for the meeting. He went to the men's store and purchased a beautiful suit and two red and black power ties. In a most obsessive mood he even picked out some delicately made socks to make himself feel sexy underneath. His underwear purchase echoed the socks. "I dressed to be attractive at least to me."

At the conference he sat at the bar, trying to remember how flirting was done. He thought of his other affair. It would be so much easier if they were together right now, but that would not be a real date. He had dressed to the nines and looked like the multi million dollar business he ran. The wine tasted delicious and calmed his nerves. His insides were grumbling as he struck up conversations with different people at the bar.

Everything seemed to work the way it was supposed to. His conversational skills were still there. He knew all the appropriate chit-chat. The drinks flowed. The atmosphere was just right, and he himself could feel the sexiness caressing his own feet. It was his first date, and in his competitive mind, he was winning. He was, well, at least ahead in the game. As everything played out, he made all of the appropriate moves. It worked well. An attractive individual invited the man upstairs and then made the excuse that the hotel room was being shared. The man picked up on his cue, stating that his room was available.

The two went to the man's room and began a sexual romp filled with intense passion. The hugging and kissing, the ripping off of each other's clothes, the smells of body sweat and sweet colognes and perfumes filled the moment. The man was in ecstasy. He had conquered this moment of being on the scene once again. He still knew how to pick up someone at a bar. He still knew how to pleasure someone sexually. On the rebound life was providing him exactly what he was seeking. In the dating game, he was winning.

As the sexual movements moved to the softness of the bed and the passion became more heated, the man began to think of his ex-spouse. Then it happened. There was absolutely no erection. There was nothing down there except the smallest piece of flesh anyone could imagine or not imagine. There was not the slightest evidence of arousal. There was not even a hint of being excited. The man did everything mentally possible to arouse the sleeping penis, but the more he thought, the less attention it gave to performing its function even slightly. Even his sexual partner whom he had conquered in this game of fantasy tried to arouse the dormant flesh. Nothing happened. There was absolutely no activity whatsoever. It was the smallest dick in the world. The man did everything else to pleasure the partner, but it was obvious that he was not going to perform this night. "I had the smallest dick in the world."

The morning brought its own distant one-night stand good-byes. They would never have to face each other again. Fortunately, his own member would not have to face the humiliation of having to perform tricks later like a caged circus lion in order to try and save face. The memory of the night was forever etched in his mind. It was his own situation comedy. He, the proud sexual master of many, had been reduced to the embarrassment of not even a tinge of action. He pictured the comedy before the heavens with everyone laughing louder than the laugh track.

He couldn't tell his friends, and when he thought of the whole incident, it made even him laugh. What a great situation comedy it had been. The irony of God placing the man in his own laughter had to be for a healing purpose. If he ever admitted it to anyone, he would run the risk of being his own laughingstock. He knew, though, that he could proceed with life, and he did.

Maintaining his special affair, and never mentioning his loss of erection to anyone, six months later he entered into an adulterous relationship with a major stockholder. Very private and very discreet, he found there was absolutely no problem with his manhood at all. His erection was erect, and the relationship satisfied his sexual needs and pleasures. This relationship was a fantasy fulfilled, and he was fit for the task. Once again, he remembered "where there is no gentleman, there is no lady." He was once again the pleasure master.

Then, when things seemed just right in his life, he was notified of the death of one of his ex-in-laws. He felt the strongest need to attend this funeral. Somewhere deep in his psyche still lay hidden the thought that perhaps a reconciliation of at least the friendship would occur. He knew that his spouse was involved already with someone else, but it did not hamper his fantasy that somehow they could return to the point of friendship with at least a glimpse of the intimacy they once shared.

It was not to be. He held his composure for as long as he could or at least until the very end. Then it happened. He realized the immensity of his own personal loss as he saw the casket lowered into the ground. He had suffered the rudeness of ex-in-laws calling the new lover by the man's name.

An ex-sister-in-law came into the kitchen to get some spaghetti for the new beau but mistakenly began to complain about having to fix this plate of food for the beau except that she called him by the name of the previous spouse. The man was standing next to the stove until the sister-in-law realized her gaffe. He heard the whispers behind his back. Even an ex-shared friend called him a cry baby in a futile attempt to assuage his hurt feelings. Weeping and sobbing in the solitude and loneliness of his car and feelings, he saw himself. I am the smallest dick in the world.

> Before all things: God does not heal *el pendejismo,* the quality of being a stupid ass. God does not heal it because humanity chooses to be that at times. If there were ever a definition of this word, it would be a picture of me. I went to the funeral of an ex-in-law, and participated in the same stupid game my "ex" has played with me for years. Why did I come here? Did I come here so that my feelings can be played with again forcing me to see the happiness of the new lover? Was it so that my "ex" can live in the illusion that everything is fine between us and that my heart does not hurt?
>
> I hate my "ex", but nevertheless, I am the *pendejo . . . pendejo* for coming here, *pendejo* for my love, *pendejo* for my feelings . . . *pendejo, pendejo, pendejo.* This whole thing is too staged and too shallow. My "ex" wants me to approve of everything without ever apologizing for what has been done to me. I want absolutely noth-

ing more to do with my ex-spouse. My "ex" does not want to admit to the hurt which I have suffered, but not even that fact is something new. My "ex" has never cared about my feelings. Why would I think that care would be a factor now?

I am a *pendejo*. It is so time to move on with my lonely life. At the interment, I saw my whole life going down into the earth with that casket. I will not be a part of this shallow self-righteous play anymore. Now, I hate my ex-spouse. My "ex" walked away without even caring or asking about how my life has been or is. My "ex" walked away thinking I approve of the way I have been treated. I do not. Here it is years later, and nothing has changed. After all these years, nothing has changed.

Pendejismo is the only thing God cannot cure or heal because humanity chooses it. I chose wrongly. This will happen no more. In my own situation comedy, I had the smallest dick in the world. Here in real life, after all my tears and affection at this funeral, I am the smallest dick in the world. No more!

PASTORAL RESPONSE

It is an incredible reality of life that too many times we justify our own actions and beliefs in order not to have to face our own errors. Christianity is not difficult, but it does demand an impeccable and unrelenting self-honesty which is rarely lived if even attempted. It demands a daily self-examination of one's relationship with the Almighty and is given human situations in order to gauge that relationship. The Scriptures are beautiful in their teaching that we are called into human relationship. Those relationships give ample evidence of how we relate to the Divine. The Scriptures are not shy about our relationship with God having its focus on how we relate to one another, especially the poor (cf. Matt 25:31–46; Luke 10:29–37; Mark 10:43–44; Luke 16:19–31).

When divorce occurs, it is evident that the rupture in the relational aspect of life and therefore with God is blatantly obvious. Jesus in the Gospels has taught that in order to love another human being one must love oneself. We know that this is a difficult thing to do. Loving oneself has to admit to the positives and negatives in one's life.

The husband had great difficulty recovering his self-honesty. As much as he would later blame his ex-spouse for the same peccadilloes of infidelity, he never made the connection that his own adultery was completely in defiance of what he had promised before the altar of God.

He could not see that the other undisclosed affairs were adulterous. His warped sense of what is a gentleman (one who does not disclose his sexual activity outside of marriage) and what is a lady (the one with whom the man has had sex outside of his marriage) flew in the face of his own marriage vows. His *pendejismo* is evident before the marriage ever took place. His pride in his own clever deception warped his own understanding of what he promised. He believed in his heart that he was a good spouse, a good Christian man living faithfully in the marriage. He saw no wrong in his personal Christian life even though it was truly rife with more than one adulterous affair.

There is a beautiful story in the gospels of a rich young man who comes to the Lord seeking to inherit eternal life (Mark 10:17–31). He is a proud young man who has many possessions. He is not ashamed about who he is or how he lives his life. He knows that he is a spiritual man. He believes in his heart that he has lived exactly as the Lord God has required of him. When he seeks Jesus out he comes to the Lord in self-honesty and belief that he has tried his best to live a life in compliance with the Scriptures.

His question to Jesus is one of spiritual desire. It is the eternal quest in every believer to desire to live in eternal union with God. As a rich young man, he has made his business decisions so that he would be financially wealthy. He is gauging his spiritual costs in the same manner as his personal business life. As a successful businessman, he knows that success is not achieved without hard work and dedication. He knows that in business there are gains and losses. He understands that in order for the business to succeed, he has had to take certain risks, accept certain restrictions on his lifestyle, be attuned to the needs of his customers, and apply common sense to life. He is a rich young man with many possessions because he has earned them.

The rich young man does not see any visible difference in his spiritual life. In his spiritual life, in order for him to succeed, he has had to take certain risks of keeping the Sabbath a part of his business. He has had to tithe acknowledging that his blessings have come from the Almighty. In his spiritual life, he has had to accept certain restrictions on his lifestyle. He has lived perfectly the 613 laws of the Torah as a faithful and devout Jewish man of the covenant. In his spiritual life, he has restricted the operating hours of his successful business because of the covenant demands from the Jewish law. In his spiritual life, he has also been attuned to the needs of God. Like a businessman who knows what pleases his customers, the rich young man also knows what pleases his Maker. Business acumen has not failed him in his spiritual life. It has enhanced his understanding that the Lord, like a customer, would also like to be pleased. It is his behavior that he offers to please God.

The rich young man is not ignorant. If he were ignorant of life, he would have lost all of his riches years ago. It is his business savvy which has brought him the prosperity he now enjoys. In his spiritual life, there is no difference. God has been with him through all things. He is not blind to the blessings he has received from the Almighty, and he is not ignorant of the incredible debt he owes to the source of those blessings. He has lived his life according to what God has asked of him. Still, he senses within his soul that is not enough. It is his spiritual common sense which is at play when he comes to Jesus with his question of what he needs to have eternal life.

Something spiritual within him understands that he is lacking in some aspect. He cannot name what he lacks, but his soul feels the lacking. His possessions have come to define him and eventually will possess him. Spiritually, he also feels well defined and very comfortable in his relationship with God.

There is, however, a nagging itch within him that perhaps he still lacks that one spiritual object which can guarantee him eternal life. As a spiritual businessman with great common sense, he asks the question hoping that he could have an edge, a businesslike spiritual edge, over life and perhaps even over God. He is not a greedy unbeliever. He is a faithful practitioner who has done well in life. His spiritual question is the result of a lived faith. There is no hidden motive behind his questioning. His question is honest. It follows the pattern of his life. It follows the pattern of what has made him a rich young man.

As the drama unfolds Jesus makes an interesting statement about goodness. The Lord refuses to accept or be defined by the human concept of goodness. He understands that people will apply to him a human understanding of what they perceive as good, just, and right, but knowing himself he can hear the prophet Isaiah ringing in his ears: "So are my ways higher than your ways" (Isa 55:9b). From the very beginning, the Lord is intent not to deal with the rich young man as if he were the young man's customer flattered and charmed so as to procure a sale or deal. He will deal with the young man on God's terms and return to the original brokerage of the covenant: "I will be their God and they shall be my people" (Jer 31:31–34).

As the young man begins his honest question as to secure his place in eternity, Jesus responds with very relational aspects of the covenant. It is noted that the most important commandment is not even mentioned: "I am the Lord your God . . . you shall have no other gods before me" (Exod 20:1–3). As Jesus proceeds to let him know of his obligations to humanity, the young man is elated as he realizes that for all of his life he has been faithful. If he has done all of this, then why is the soul still nagging for an answer which will sate the void of doubt tugging at his heart? He professes his verifiable actions to the Lord and proudly states his fidelity since his youth. His choices have been choices for God, and his commitment has never swayed.

It is no mistake that the Lord lovingly looks upon the young man at this moment, because it is his desire to evangelize him lovingly. Jesus sees into the heart of his child and as a parent wanting the best desires that the young man know God and his ways and not just know about God and his ways. Lovingly he begins to challenge the young man to know firsthand the majesty of who God is. He is not a commodity to be bought and sold. He is not an item one purchases with fidelity. He is not a thing. God is love, and loves him. God has a relationship with his child before he ever saw the light of day (Psalm 139:13-16). God desires a loving response not the issuance of a purchase receipt.

Now on God's terms Jesus tells the young man what discipleship costs. It costs the very first commandment: I am the Lord your God and you shall have no other gods before me (Exod 20:1–3). To go and sell and give all to the poor in order to come back and follow Jesus is an incredible request.

It was a request that this honest businessman summed up and calculated very quickly realizing that his money meant too much to him. He walked away sad realizing that his possessions possessed him. His money was his god. He in all of his striving to keep the commandments was finding it impossible to live the very first one. Very lovingly, Jesus has reminded the young man that all his self-righteousness servitude is worthless before the righteousness of the Almighty.

The husband had spent the years of his marriage in a façade of respectability fancying himself the perfect husband. He could stand before the Lord in his prayer time and count the deeds he had done for others.

As a Christian believer, he was not ashamed to teach classes of catechism, to profess his baptismal vows loudly, and to give God praise in public. Presuming the forgiveness of God, he wrote off his affairs in blatant self-justification. The divorce forced him into a new relationship not only with other people but with God himself. Seeing himself in his own situation comedy brought home the hard reality of his own personal loss. God still lovingly was calling him to go and settle his affairs and then come follow him. Like the rich young man in the story or like the characters in his television comedies, or like his rebound sexual encounter, the spouse has found that his pretensions at living his own goodness are worthless if they are not rooted in the very first of the commandments. Like the rich young man, the husband found that it was too difficult to stop his affairs, give his successful business to the needs of the poor, and be faithful to God first because his affairs, sexual and financial, had come to define him as the riches in the story defined the rich young man.

Fidelity is not found in spousal relationships based on human understanding. Fidelity is rooted in our relationship with God. It is not that we have loved God; rather it is that God has loved us first (1 John 4:10). If the rich young man had loved God above his money, he would have found the beginnings of eternal life in this life. If the husband had loved God faithfully first, he would have found fidelity in the marriage. The rich young man walked away knowing that all his deeds counted for nothing because in all honesty he had not lived the very first of what he was asked to do out of love for God. The husband found himself alone with his human follies because he had not lived the very first of what he was asked to do out of love for God. Neither one was capable of letting those things go because their possessions/affairs possessed them.

The Lord broke the young man's arrogance with the truth. The Lord broke the husband's arrogance as well. The funeral of the family member caused the husband to stew in his anger at how he had been cheated by life. The truth, however, is that his own cheating had cheated life. Neither story states whether the rich young man or the current divorced spouse ever came back to the Lord, but both of these men have had their lives radically challenged to return to the fidelity to have no gods before the Living God. The Living God lovingly challenges us to self-honesty that we might love God faithfully.

A PRAYER OF RECONCILIATION

My soul is in pain,
blurring good times and bad times.
My tears never cease.

Like the sky's rain clouds,
my soul in ebony sin
bathing in self-hate.

I struggle to live,
and, just when I think I heal,
I bleed once again.

Soy tu Creador.
En el vientre, yo te ví.
Quiero besarte,
porque eres mi hijo,
porque eres mi amor.

Ví tu depresión.
tus lagrimas me duelen.
Lloré contigo.
En mis manos estarás.
Siempre te he amado.

8

I Am Really Concerned About You

GUILT IS ONE OF the most powerful feelings that affects our human lives. Before we realize it, guilt weaves its subtle emotion into our thinking usually with a pseudo-attempt at trying to evoke some sense of remorse from us which we are probably not at the moment ready to offer. Guilt, being an emotion, has no moral value, and like all emotions vacillates from positive to negative responses. Because of its past history, however, guilt brings with it many negative connotations. Submitting to guilt can force us to realize what our responsibilities truly are and even awake within us the desire to change some behaviors. Conscious behavioral changes can even lead to appropriation of the behavior (ownership). When behavioral changes are owned and appropriated (made mine), then guilt is no longer the initiating factor in how we live our lives. In some instances guilt pricks our consciences out of its stagnation and demands a behavioral choice and response to people or situations. Eventually one must ask the obvious question. Am I making these changes out of guilt or because I want to make them? The answer determines the healthiness of future behavior.

The goal should always be appropriation, but sadly many people operate out of guilty feelings rather than seeing the opportunity to a healthier life that behavioral changes even begun out of guilt could bring. Always operating out of guilt is certainly unhealthy because it illustrates there is no appropriation, no ownership of one's life. Guilt has the power to allow us to cede over our life choices to another human being. It has the tendency to force us to live by appearances rather than in honesty. We do things motivated by what others think rather than what our hearts and consciences instruct us to do. We become more interested in what seems to be the perception people have of us rather than our own developed and growing self image.

144

Those who continually do some good for another, because they feel guilty if they do not, have not appropriated the "why" of what is being done. They simply act with unwillingness to view a broader picture. Doing good does not flow naturally but has to be prodded like cattle into actually moving forward in life (Matt 25:31–46). As sons and daughters of a loving God, goodness should flow naturally from our beings (Matt 25:37–40). The truth exists, however, that even non-action at times flows just as naturally without any remorse (Matt 25:31–46). Like the Pharisees of old, people acting out of guilt with no appropriation of the good, perform acts without the heart as to why these acts are necessary. Guilt makes empty rituals. It is a faith without works, empty and lifeless (Jas 2), even though it had the potential to be appropriated, and so becoming full and life-giving.

If there is no permanent move toward behavioral changes, then the actions performed become merely moments used to assuage one's guilt. Guilt finds its way into human love relationships. Assuaging one's guilt does not look to the good of the other. Assuagement is not based in love of God, self, or the other. Assuaging one's guilt is a selfish act requiring no change in behavior. Although the appearance of a good deed may seem outwardly kind and altruistic, it is as empty and filthy as whitened sepulchers when done out of guilt. Eventually the stench of assuagement is as putrid as any open tomb (Matt 23:27). The more one engages him or herself with another, even God, the more one is forced to examine and re-examine constantly the healthiness of those relationships. The frequency with which this examination is done will motivate one to change not out of guilt but out of love for the other. With God, it is called prayer.

Do I love as I am loved? Do I forgive as I am forgiven? Do my actions reflect the intimacy of my relationships with other people? Do I share? Do I give and receive with equal measure? Is my relationship with other people and God a reciprocal experience? Do my loving actions flow naturally? Do my non-actions, my refusal to love, flow just as naturally?

Guilt forces us to recognize the rupture in the married relationship, and at the least, we may hold some culpability. Culpability is one of the least favorite avenues to broach. Because of our human nature, we avoid culpability because it demands that we look upon our brokenness in life. There are actual instances in life when things are our fault even in relationships. When relationships begin to deteriorate, more often than not in an unhealthy manner, culpability is ignored as blame is assigned, distancing oneself from any of the blame. The twofold nature of culpability comes down to a simple question. Whose fault is it? This question, though innocent enough, has a dark side to it as well. The unspoken part of this question is the quiet statement: I am not to blame. Especially in marital matters this question immediately distances one party from the action. The two that initially became one become two again and not in a pleasant manner. The obsession to blame the other spouse for the minutest of indiscretions or rude statements refuses to acknowledge one's own culpability.

It is noteworthy that real guilt and genuine culpability, because of their negative connotations, have been sorely ignored in our society. We have been conditioned to excuse our behavior usually at the expense of blaming someone else or some situation. Our failures in life are seen as the result of someone else's doings rather than an honest recognition of the consequences of our behavior. Rare are the moments when we step up to the plate and announce that the painful situations of my life are usually the consequences of my own behavior or misbehavior. We find it almost abhorrent to admit that in all possibility we may be guilty of giving into evil in our own life. Refusing to see our own brokenness, we refuse to see our own culpability. In broken marriages, it is too painful to look at the situation objectively and see that "I" too have some responsibility for the rupture. It hurts too much to admit that I played some part in the shattering of vows.

Divorce is the banquet for all of these emotional factors (guilt, culpability, appropriation) to have their feast. The rupture of the marriage is the blanket for the emotional picnic to begin. The feast of emotions begins with each bringing a picnic basket ready to serve the broken lovers until the divorced are sated beyond their limits. Broken lovers partake of every emotion in sight feasting until all they can do is lie on their backs unable to move forward or get up from the blanket. They are so full after eating every emotion available, they cannot move. They are bloated with the gases of their emotions and feelings of their broken lives. Both feel miserable.

Divorce does not seek healing. Its purpose is to separate. Blaming is not uncommon in any divorce situation as the peccadilloes of each party are brought to light. Hateful curses and real statements mix with every evil memorable moment of the relationship are re-lived to the point of exhaustion. Broken lovers look for reasons as to why the breakup has occurred, but usually they look to the actions of the other party in order to locate the reasons for the breakup. Broken lovers are experts at remembering and naming the omissions and commissions that the other party has done. They usually come up short, though, when having to name their own culpability in the failed relationship. Broken lovers feast on blaming the other party even years later. It is not uncommon that when recalling the divorce, one ex-spouse will immediately focus on the sins of the other as if the incident had happened yesterday. With a lack of healing, the emotions are so raw, even years later, that it is not uncommon for a frightful bitterness to couch and coat the nasty comments that will be uttered to anyone who will listen.

Guilt in these situations is never healthy. It is used more as a weapon ready to discharge ammunition at the other party. Guilt is used to make the other party feel bad or at least irresponsible. It is used without the intention of having the other party change his or her behavior. Guilt or guilt trips are used to make the other party hurt. In broken lover situations, guilt is not used for behavioral change and has no intention of allowing the other person to use it as an opportunity for growth. Guilt statements are used to destroy the psyche of the others and to remind him/her of his/her sinfulness in the relationship.

Guilt becomes the instrument for blame. As blaming begins the breakup of the marriage, guilt becomes the tool for asserting and assigning blame to the other person. Guilt, however, is not used in any positive ways. It is used to shame the dignity of the other person but not with the intention that the other party will change behavior. Guilt is used simply to hurt the emotional state of the other person. With usually an intensity of hate and anger accompanying the guilt-laden assertions, one party devastates the other, reminding him/her of the obvious which cannot be seen: the other partner is the reason for the breakup of this marriage.

As each sin is re-lived, reiterated, and unforgiven, guilt shames the other party for how he or she has failed to live in the relationship as a mutual partner instead of thinking of him-or herself and personal needs. Guilt is used to illustrate the sins of avarice and greed but only of the other party and without any care or concern for change. Divorce does not remember good times and uses guilt to declare before everyone only the bad times.

In many instances there is a volume of truth spoken when lovers fight. The difficulty is that neither one of them can hear it. Their ears are closed to hearing or integrating any culpability because of the source from which it comes. The hurt of the divorce, the bleeding of the dead marriage, and the stench of the decaying relationship prevent both partners from being free enough to remove themselves objectively from the situation in order to hear and see any truth which may be forthcoming.

To a devastated spouse, truth is indiscernible at this moment. In the heat of the arguments, everything the other party says is suspect. Their words like their broken vows are simply lies. The pain of divorce will always focus on the lies of the marriage. It becomes very difficult to hear any truth from the lips of an ex-spouse because everything is now seen through the lens of broken vows. It is a liar who is speaking, and the emotional scars are there to prove it.

How can this person tell me of my life when he lied about fidelity and permanence? How can this person tell me what I need to change in my life when he lied about how he would live his life with me? How can this person say he has my interest at heart when he never did in the marriage? How is it possible that my wellbeing is an issue now when nothing in the marriage indicated it was ever an issue at all? How can this person sanctimoniously walk away from the sanctity of what was promised before the Almighty? How can this person who lied to me and God now tell me what is the truth of my life? How can this person blame the breakup on me without ever realizing he did not marry himself?

These and similar questions never find satisfactory resolutions. They are asked countless times in the mind of the divorced. When a divorced person recalls memories which continue to plague him/her, any mix of these questions will come forward evoking different responses depending on the level and intensity of the current moment. From extreme grief to extreme anger, these questions touch a broad spectrum of available emotions. In their minds, as well, they hear the voice of their "ex" belittling and badgering him/her once again. Their peccadilloes are replayed over and over as they look for places where the marriage went wrong.

The divorced hear the voice of the "ex" reminding him/ her of how incapable of love he/she is. Divorced individuals begin to question themselves in all areas: physically, sexually, religiously, emotionally, spiritually. They hear once again the guilt trips, and the words begin to sting as the divorced mentally wrestle with what is truth and what is venom. The arguments are re-lived again and again.

In rapid succession, the mind replays horrible memories of words and moments. Even in the most abusive relationships, when separation is more than necessary, the words and memories leave such a deep devastating wound that they can bleed for years to come. Hurting words sting at the core of being causing an array of doubts which never cease and are always raw. Raw doubts are literally the only things that last until death do them part.

In the barrage of words and guilt, in the devastating memories that eat at the divorced, there is the painful reality that an inkling of truth does exist in those barrages. There is the hurting hurt that the verbal reminder of offenses, no matter how offensive they seem to be, holds a kernel of truth which eventually needs to be addressed. Hurting statements gnaw at the soul begging for a discerning examination because they were not stated out of a vacuum. They came from a past relationship, a broken one at that, but a relationship nonetheless. The statements deserve examination far away from the emotions of the divorce. Although the source may come from an unpleasant broken relationship laced in guilt trips, there still exists the need to explore and challenge one's behavior for growth to occur.

The sadness of the divorce, however, rarely allows a person to examine the veracity of the statements of an "ex" because the breakup is a physical reminder of the blatant lie of the vows. Whatever issues from the mouth of an ex-spouse may be true, but the words, concepts, and even attempts at healing remain suspect because the lived reality points to physical separation. There is no having and holding until death do us part. Divorce says we " killed the marriage; therefore, let us part."

CASE STUDY

The couple had been together for almost eighteen years. They had married in their twenties with all of the idealism of making a good marriage. They saw themselves as the couple who would conquer all of the problems of marriage. They were right for each other and not ashamed of flaunting to others their love and affection for each other. They always remarked they were made for each other. They talked of how they would spend their golden years in happiness. There were dreams of opening up a bed and breakfast with crazy Tarot readings for guests. They reminded other people they were a couple by being publicly affectionate with each other even if it was not appropriate like at the symphony or theater or on a bus. They liked to play together, dancing, partying, and always were very respectful of their sensuousness with each other. They avoided issues when arguments arose and passed them off as just part of life and marriage. They could be the life at a party, but if they were angry with each other, no one wanted to get caught in the middle or taking sides.

Their marriage proved to be too demanding for each of them. They both suffered with bouts of infidelity. Their reconciliations became half-hearted as both sought others as outside influences for their inner relationship. It was inevitable for the marriage to end. Many had predicted the fall, but not the couple. They held on to the relationship even in its lie as long as they could until eventually one partner had had enough. It was over and no amount of pleading, begging, whining, or crying could change the situation. The mind had determined it was over.

The divorce proceeded as any other. No children were involved. The hurt and devastation was that divorce, unlike almost everything else in their relationship, was not mutual. They had spent years deciding as best as they could to make decisions together, but the divorce, like all pre-arranged, pre-planned events, was the desire of one spouse. One party wanted out. This person had discussed the decision with other friends (not mutual ones), planned the moment (the here, when, and now), and carefully executed everything on schedule.

It was an interesting plan. Everything had to be done before the New Year. Everything had to be done before the new millennium. The year 2000 could not begin with this relationship extending itself into the newness of what the world was hoping to celebrate. Although everything was carefully laid out for a good execution of the plan, it was also evident the party did not have the fortitude or courage to carry it out. The plan was a simple one. Accept all the guilt. Do not engage in conversation. Stay firm in the resolve to end the marriage as quickly and quietly as possible.

For whatever reason, but probably because at some level they actually did love each other knowing that they grew up together in this relationship, the plan was executed and fulfilled by the other party. The initial party began with some nonsensical verbiage about needing to go somewhere other than the bedroom to talk about things. The other spouse, coming in from a long day of work and travel, just wanted to be intimate with the spouse but started to hear the shakiness of the beloved's voice and began to finish the thought processes that were unfolding. The initiator never asked for a divorce. When it was all said and done, the initiator never said a word beyond wanting to go somewhere else to talk. The other spouse realized what was being asked (divorce) and stated it to the initiator who simply nodded to a barrage of questions coming from the other spouse. "You mean you want out? You mean you want a divorce? You mean you do not want to be together anymore?" Simple nods and one occasional "it's not you; it's me" was the demand that what God had joined needed to be untied, put asunder. In pride and anger, in humiliation and fear, the other spouse left the house never to return. It seemed so simple. The plan had worked. Divorce had been started and would be achieved.

The husband never returned to the house but found himself living in a nightmarish hell of feelings and emotions. Each memory confronted him with the failure of relationship. Each room of thought contained the furniture of undoing: chairs of lies, beds of infidelity, sofas of adultery, tables of selfishness, lamps of darkness. Each room of memory reminded him of his failure to love and marked at a deeper emotional and psychological level, his failure to be loved. Psychologically, he found himself at points of suicide. His alcoholism became more dominant in his life. If he did not take his life by physical act, then he would indulge himself in the taking of his life by his addiction. His divorce imprisoned him beyond all telling.

His friends were sick of hearing about it. Some friends had sided with the initiator. His mind could hear the voices of those nay-sayers who had scoffed at the relationship from the beginning. His memory played and replayed the leaving scene throughout the day, verily throughout the days. He delved into work so as to hide his hurt. He suppressed his tears until he was in the privacy of his own home. There he would cry a man's tears asking whoever was out there when no one was there if this could be rectified. Tears at night hidden from everyone marred his moods, took away his laughter, and turned all joy into sorrow. There was nothing to live for anymore.

His clergyman, sympathetic at the beginning, eventually ridiculed him (thinking it was time to laugh) by stating the obvious: you got dumped by a lover. He knew this was only half true but cruel to hear put so bluntly. This was his spouse, his beloved, the one he had cherished, with whom he had shared his bed. His spouse was not some cheap lover. His spouse was the one he had loved.

A male friend took him to a stripper bar to cheer him up. His friend told him to sit at the stripper's table to watch the show, forget his worries, and see that life goes on. He sat at the table in front of the stripper drinking his beer while his friend went to say hello to others and get more beer. He sat and cried drinking his beer and mentally re-living his sorrows. Eventually his depression was so intense, his tears so visible the stripper asked him to move to somewhere else because no one could concentrate on the dancing and money was being lost. His depression over the loss of his beloved was even bad for the stripper's business. He cried that much harder, never moved, and the show was postponed until he left the bar hours later.

After a nervous breakdown with suicide portending to be a viable option and hovering over him like a vulture awaiting its prey, he sought help. By accident through his church, he encountered workshops which spoke of healing from divorce. He availed himself of what he could and began a healing process. He educated himself about his feelings and emotions. He found a spiritual counselor who helped him walk through the feelings, the emotions, the vices, the fears.

A year and a half after the divorce, he began a relationship with a beautiful woman. She had always been a fantasy of his and now a new relationship became a reality. He missed his ex-spouse, but the new relationship returned him to the dignity he had diminished by his self-afflictions in the aftermath of the divorce. This new relationship, however, had started as a fantasy and pleased him. It was an obvious reality to him that the relationship would never achieve the union of what he had had in his marriage, but it gave him confidence and pleasure. He would often say to himself, "I am a man again."

Then one day out of the blue he received a phone call from his "ex." The "ex" would be passing through on an airplane layover and wanted to know if there was time for a quick lunch visit. By this time the man had healed significantly, but the phone call gave him a tumble beyond his own imagining. He already had plans for a date with his new fantasy. They had progressed in the relationship to very intimate levels. He did not want to cancel the date, and he did not want to miss the chance to see the one he truly loved. He still was in love with his "ex." He still held somewhere in the recesses of his thoughts that maybe, just maybe, they would re-unite. He had never told his "ex" about his fantasy relationship. It was his business and no one else's. He knew his "ex" was in another relationship too, but that did not matter. Other couples had gotten back together; why couldn't they?

He took some time to respond trying to get the best out of the situation. He knew in his heart he was still healing. His "ex" could not define him so easily anymore. He would not cancel his date. He would not tell his "ex" about the date. He would meet the "ex," go to lunch, and drop the "ex" back at the airport a little earlier than the take-off schedule so that his own rendezvous with his new fantasy lover would not be compromised. Things went well. He even took the "ex" to a favorite Chinese restaurant they had enjoyed years ago. Then the lies began.

"I am really concerned for you," said the ex-spouse.

The man did not know how to respond. All he could think of was the cowardly breakup. His mind raced to say things, but he did not want this episode to be volatile, though his whole heart was awash in anger and rage. He wanted to scream across the table, "You fucking bitch!" but he held those words and like a pig slurped his egg drop soup so as not to curse. He could see himself eating the soup as if he were ten years old, not being able to eat it fast enough so guilty with thought, that others could hear his mental screams.

I have had a bad time, he said.

Yes, me too.

No, I mean I almost had a nervous breakdown.

Yes, I know what you mean. Times were hard, and I ended up doing some stupid personal stuff after our breakup. I want you to know though that I am really concerned about you. Not that we would ever get together again, but I am concerned.

The man shut down. His mind turned toward his date that night. This lunch was hurting. "Concerned about me?" he thought. Were you concerned when you muted to me you wanted a divorce? Were you concerned about me when you made me mouth your insecurities? Were you concerned about me when you never even wanted to salvage the friendship? Were you concerned about me when I bled from my heart or are we just here to echo your hurts? Echo your hurts sounds like the marriage we left. Then as if the sun arose from its night sleep, the man realized what was going on. There was no concern for his wellbeing. This was the same pattern of the marriage. This lunch was to talk about the spouse and the spouse's well being. The man recognized his progress in healing and refused to be engaged in this pity party. He did not want to hear about the emotional suffering of his "ex." His "ex" had caused the suffering by desiring the divorce, by wanting out of the relationship. If the "ex" had suffered, so be it, for the "ex" sought the divorce in the first place and now had to live with the consequences.

Then as clear as the night follows the day, the man became aware of the eternal lie: I am really concerned about you. The "ex" could not even hear or relate to the pain of the man, always masking his pain with a justification of "how I have suffered through this as well." Never did the ex-spouse acknowledge the pain or hurt of the man. Never did the "ex" feel genuine compassion for the man. Never did any type of true concern for the man manifest itself. It was simply the same old self-centered egotistical rubbish of eighteen years of living together. "I am really concerned about you" had translated into "let me talk about me."

The man recognized the lie, saw through the self-centeredness, changed the subject to extended family matters, and waited for time to return the spouse to the airport. His date would be much more enjoyable. The "ex" would walk quietly away justifying in her own mind that things were still amicable between the two, and what a pleasant lunch was had by all. At the airport, the man gave his "ex" a manuscript he had been working on, asking his ex-spouse to proof it, knowing it contained material and information they shared.

Just mail it to me.

No here take it with you. I want you to have it too.

The man knew it was a waste of time. It was the same lie. I am really concerned about you meant whatever is important to you is not that important to me. "Just mail it to me." The "ex" took the manuscript reluctantly, folded it, put it in the carry-on bag and walked through the terminal gates. It would be close to two years before the manuscript would be returned with commentary. The "ex" returned it personally, but it was still obvious to the man that it had probably not been read except in excerpts. It did not matter. He was freer now and knew that never had there been a genuine concern for him, either in the divorce or the marriage. His night after the airport drop off ended in sexual ecstasy. He was a man again.

PASTORAL RESPONSE

In the Gospel of St. Luke, chapter 15, we are given three most beautiful stories of forgiveness. All three are classic Lucan examples of his own conversion process. It must have been a wonderful moment in the life of St. Luke when he was baptized. His love for Jesus Christ spilled over into a Gospel for the lover of God (Theophilus). His stories are written for those who love God. He has infused into his narrative of the life of Jesus every aspect of his own baptism as a Christian man. He tells us the story of Jesus Christ through the lens of baptism eyes. Rich in the blessings of baptism, he knows that he has one foot in the kingdom of heaven already, and the other foot is in the kingdom of heaven. Therefore, nothing in his life escapes the love of Jesus Christ. So peculiar to Luke is the joy of his baptism, the reading of this Gospel clothes us in the joy of the Holy Spirit, singing canticles of praise, touching the joy of the eighth day of creation, bathing us in Mary's fiat, letting us rest in prayer, and cleansing us with forgiveness.

His is the Gospel of forgiveness. Like a good thief stealing into heaven, forgiveness is the grace of crucifixion (Luke 23:39–43). Forgiveness being one of his favorite themes, St. Luke tells us three marvelous stories of being lost: a lost sheep, a lost coin, and verily a lost family (Luke 15). It is important to remember that Jesus tells these stories because of the hard-heartedness of the Pharisees and scribes. They see Jesus eating and conversing with sinners and tax collectors, and they are appalled at his behavior. His behavior is not in keeping with the ritual purity he should be upholding as a good Jewish man and rabbi. Jesus always attentive to their hearts of stone tells them three lost stories. Sheep, coins, family. Lost is lost.

The first story of the lost sheep is simple mathematics. It is, however, not good business practices. Jesus poses a question to the Pharisees as to which of them having a hundred sheep would not leave the ninety-nine in search of the lost one. Although this sounds like a simple rhetorical question, it is not. He does not wait for a human answer. He plods through their thickness giving them the divine answer. But if we dissect the problem at a deeper level, we find a shocking conclusion. When the Lord asks the question, he already knows his answer and theirs, and they are vastly different.

Jesus' problem with the sheep is that the human answer is not the divine one. Luke records the divine answer, but the human one is left in the hardness of the pharisaical heart. The human answer to Jesus' question is no one. No one would leave ninety-nine sheep unprotected to go in search of one lost sheep. It is not good business practice. It makes no monetary sense. One can almost hear the echo of the Passion: better for one to die than the whole nation. Humanly speaking, it is not cost productive to search out one sheep at the risk of coming back to find that you have lost ninety-nine. No one in his right business sense would ever think that this would be a viable option.

Knowing now that the human answer to Jesus' question is no one, Jesus then goes on to paint an idyllic picture of a shepherd embracing his trembling bleating sheep, placing it on his shoulders, and carrying it back to the fold. And the moral is: rejoicing angels in heaven dancing unto the wee hours of eternity, for a sinner has repented and returned to the grace of God. The human answer, however, remains the same: no one. If the answer is no one then it begs the question of why.

I frequently ask first communicants as they prepare for their first reconciliation using this Gospel, "why did that shepherd go to look for that one lost sheep?" That shepherd had ninety-nine other sheep, plenty to take care of. Why in the world would he leave that many sheep unprotected to go and look for one little lost sheep? There are various pat answers which are half right, but it usually takes awhile before one sheepish child raises his/her hand and says, 'Because it's his!' It is the divine answer. No human shepherd would do such a crazy thing. God, however, who had to shepherd his flock in spite of the human shepherds does search the lost sheep out (Ezek.34). Why? Because it is his.

Why does a woman search and sweep her house to find a coin if she still has nine left. Its precious value is not as great as the nine she still has, except that in her divine understanding, the coin is hers. It belongs to no other. She will sweep until eternity, turning on all the lights and overturning all the furniture until she finds what almost escaped her. Her reasoning is because it is hers. And the moral is: rejoicing angels in heaven dancing unto the wee hours of eternity, for a sinner has repented and returned to the grace of God.

And in the trauma and tragedy of a prodigal family, suffice it to say there was a father who had two lost sons. He had to wait until one found his senses and to plead with the other to find his. His waiting and plead- ing exemplify his reasoning: because both those boys were his.

Genuine concern for another individual has roots only in the un- derstanding of our connectedness with that other individual. Genuine concern about the safety and health of another human being has roots in love. Love always looks to the other. We cry for those whom we love. We are concerned about those to whom we are connected. Jesus' message which falls on too many deaf ears is that we are all connected, and our tears ought to be shed for all humanity. Jesus relates these three parables to people whose hearts obstinately refused to see their connectedness with sinners and tax collectors. Even love of self has its roots in loving the other: the first relationship is with God, our Creator, our Maker.

The man in the case study found it extremely difficult in his divorce to love himself. He could not relate to the Author of Life so that life be- came very unimportant to him. His tears flow because he wrongly thinks that even God could not love him. He cries out of being disconnected. His flirting with thoughts of suicide illustrates his own lack of connectedness with himself and his Maker. His desire to end life could not even let him see who had given him life. God had to break into his life. Why? Because the man was his. He belonged to God and to no other. God could leave the ninety-nine, search out his sheep, and put him into the workshop folds so that healing might occur.

Those workshops which took place long before the ex-spousal en- counter taught him the love of God once again. They taught him to dis- tinguish truth from lie, whether his or another's. Those workshops given from the brokenness of other human beings taught him to discern well genuine concern. Those workshops took his broken soul, placed it before a loving Lord who carried it back to the fold to be shepherded by the only One who is genuinely concerned for all our well being. Why? Because he was and is God's.

Divorce is not the end of life. It is the end of a marriage. It does not have the power to determine or define one's existence. Although its trag- edies and emotional scars wreak havoc upon our souls, our souls belong to God. God sweeps our messy room looking for the precious living coin who we are (1 Pet 2:5). God climbs over the hills and wastelands of adul- tery, lies, anger, and violence to embrace our bleating with his care (Song 2:8). God crosses the deserts of our abuses (emotional, physical, verbal, psychological, spiritual, and sexual) waiting for us to return to him and pleading with us to rejoice in our forgiveness. Why? Because we are his.

It is in that connectedness with God that we know forgiveness. How difficult it was for that man to rise from his suicidal options and seek help. But it did not originate from himself. He had always belonged to the Holy One, and the Spirit who intercedes for us when things are bleak (Rom 8) erupted in intercession for what belonged to the Father. The man found life, and life in abundance (John 10:10).

What of the ex spouse? A deep self-examination needs to occur here. There must be an admission of truth as to how and why the divorce took place. This never has to be done in front of the man, but in her spiritual journey, it does not behoove her to lie to herself so as to justify her wanting out of the relationship. Her guilt is evident even to an outside neutral third party. Her denial is deafening especially to herself. Denial of culpability is a strong pattern in her life, but if that self- examination ever took place, she would come to realize she belongs to the Lord too. She would realize the hurt she caused not because of the divorce but because of the dishonesty in its implementation. Her concern for her "ex" would actually become a genuine concern for him and for herself. The moral, therefore, would be: rejoicing angels in heaven dancing into the wee hours of eternity because a sinner had repented and returned to the grace of God.

A PRAYER IN DESPAIR

No light, No day, No sun, No friend,
No Joy, No hope, No song, No one,
No cushion of joy.

NO YOU.

Inside I feel you stir.
O, please Lord,
feel Me.

9

Hey, I Am Going To Be In Town

DIVORCE, THE PUBLIC CESSATION of a very private and intimate matter carries much baggage. At the time of the breakup there are hundreds of issues which cry for healing. There are a multitude of questions screaming for answers. There are reels of memories which clamor to be shown and replayed in attempts to find causes or more often to lay blame. At the time of the divorce, there are so many languages being heard from a myriad of emotions that each party is incredibly incapable of interpreting the other party's words or feelings, much less his or her own. Too much verbiage mixed with emotions explodes as a marriage ends. Too many word-laced feelings are shot as cannon balls at each other in the hopes that when the smoke clears nothing or perhaps no one will be left standing.

There is rarely an honest and realistic examination of the damage which has occurred. Divorce is not the end of life. It is the finalization of what died months ago, sometimes years before. The damage, however, of the death of the marriage lingers like the stench of death. Once that smell hits the nostrils, it is impossible ever to eradicate it from the memory. As indescribable as it is, the stench of death never leaves one who has had his or her olfactory glands penetrated by this smell. Divorce is the same as death. Its stench lingers like a rotting cadaver and permeates every aspect of living even when healing occurs at some level.

The reality of divorce is that it damages. Many parties are not even aware of how damaged they are after a divorce. They are so attuned to their own worries and problems they cannot see how their soul and spirit have been brutalized. They do not understand they walk in this world like zombies, living dead souls going through the routines of daily life but never seeing in the mirror of life how bloodied they are. They never realize how damaged they have become. It never crosses their mind that the entire episode, the marriage and the divorce, has detonated their lives. They look like the aftermath of Hiroshima.

The divorced live in the land of "if . . . only": if life would only grant them the grace to withdraw from the world to look in the mirror at their tears and cleanse their souls; if life would only grant them the grace to put everything else on hold while they combed their hair, and rebuilt their shattered dreams; if only they had a moment of grace to think of how they had been party to this devastation now ruling their lives; if they had only a chance to hear someone honestly tell them they were loved, and are still loved in this world. At this juncture of the divorce process, this is exactly what is needed: a time out.

A time out is sorely needed. The ordinary demands of life are important, but they become so draining on the soul as it tries to make sense of the roller-coaster ride of emotions it is on. Time outs are important but are not the cure. Time out gives the griever a chance to grieve. Putting life on hold should be the goal, but the everyday demands of family, job, bills, and divorce papers do not allow the grace of a time out. Time outs give the griever a chance at re-growth from a healthier perspective. Time outs allow the grieving to see how damaged they have become by the death of the marriage. Time outs rarely exist.

When a divorced person does not take time out, which is usually the case, the damage, that has been done, festers. The wound becomes that much tender. Grieving has to occur. Grieving cannot be escaped. It cannot be swept under the rug or suppressed so as not to have to deal with it. Grieving will search throughout the soul until it finds its outlet. Grieving occurs when it decides and not at the whim or desire of the divorced. The damage of the event takes on greater proportions when alcohol, drugs, or other addictions become self-medications. Because of the pressures of the day and its own demands, often grieving is relegated to late night moments of loneliness when the stark reality of absence stares one in the face.

The tears have to be shed. The anger has to be voiced even to walls with no ears. The curses have to be sworn even to an "ex" who never heard the curses in his or her presence in the marriage. The grieving has to ask all the unanswered questions: why? how come? and what now? The grieving has to confront the obvious loneliness. The pillows have to receive the moistness of tears because a death has occurred. Death hurts. With no time out, this scene is repeated over and over mentally with all the phantom memories and physically with all the wetness of salty tears raining like a relentless monsoon. Even the grieving one asks for a cessation of the grieving, but the memories pay no attention as the tsunami of emotions wreaks devastation on soul and body. The physical and mental drain on the human person is immense. Divorce is the constant daily reminder of not being loved by someone. It is the red flag which shouts to everyone who will look that here lies a damaged person, a brokenness whose human worth is questionable at best.

Time outs are essential in this process. When a divorced person is in need, it is crucial for a minister to realize the fragility of who lies before him. The divorced is a fragile child of God who believes (or at least has questioned) that not even God loves him at this moment. He/ or she is immensely immersed in the pain of what has occurred blinded to the Light of Life. Their hurt is so profound they do not know the Healer of Souls. Their spirit is so low they question why or whether they have a spirit at all.

They are damaged. They have been damaged by another human being who promised to love them beyond all imagination. They have damaged themselves by their own errors and foibles in the ruined relationship they once called marriage. They damage themselves every day in their fears and tears. They damage themselves at night in the privacy of their thoughts and anger. They damage themselves in their addictions especially the ones they attempt to hide from family, friends, and even themselves. They make fragile attempts at rebuilding without ever acknowledging the depth of their personal damage. Their desire is to be healed, to forget without forgiving, yet their relationship with the Eternal Healer is also damaged if they blame God for the consequences of their failed marriage. Their spirit is damaged to the point that it desires to play God and in a warped sense of vengeance, attempts to hurt the "ex," even to desiring pain or death.

Time outs are essential. It is very important to re-teach the value of the human person. Time outs come from friends and planning to do something for oneself. At this juncture of the process a divorced person needs to rediscover a sense of pampering oneself. We do not like to do that. We have grown so accustomed to doing for others that we feel guilty if we are called to take care of ourselves.

I encourage divorced people to try as hard as they can to do two exercises. The first one is entitled "marking the calendar." Grief is immeasurable, but healing can be charted. I ask divorcing persons to get a calendar and every day they cry, they are to mark an X on that day. If in the counseling session they have cried with me, then that day gets an X. There can be no cheating. Healing demands honesty to oneself above all else. Each day tears come, the person must mark the calendar to see his hurt outside of himself. The day he does not cry (and it does come) he marks a +. The cross is to remind him God does love him. God too is involved in this healing process of marking the calendar. God is Rock from which well-springs of water flow. God will take the tears and cleanse them with life-giving water. Marking the calendar allows the individual to see visibly that tears and memories do not need to be the sole governing factors in his or her life.

The second exercise is called pampering. We are not trained to do this well. It is a time out which begins with love of self. This allows me to love others, so that I may love the Lord with all my being. Love of self has taken on negative connotations because it has a tendency to become selfish, turning the pampered into a bragging monster. True love of self is rooted in the care of self: loving my graces and sins, growing in grace, and reducing my sinfulness. Love of self at this stage of the divorce requires a pampering time out. I ask divorcing persons to name at least three ways they can do something out of the ordinary for themselves. Name three things which are a waste of time and money. Name three things you would never do though they might be fun or at least different. I challenge the person to do them. I challenge them to pamper themselves with an ice cream cone—by themselves, without friends or family, and especially without children. I challenge them to farm the kids out to the "ex" or family members for a night and cuddle up with a good movie and home-made popcorn. I challenge them to a private bubble bath with candles and a nice Pinot Grigio. Pampering teaches us that above all else we need to love ourselves.

I remember a conference where a woman came to me beaten down. She was the saddest person in the world. She was Atlas carrying the whole world in her grief. She even made me cry. I wanted to reach inside her brain and move things around so that she might see the beauty of life. I wanted her to know that no one has the right to define a life save God, and even then God chooses to give us a free will so that we might define our lives of service for him. It was to no avail. Her grief was the grief of Ramah (Jer 40:1). Her tears were the deaths of Saul and Jonathan (2 Sam

1:23–26). Her inner screams were the voices of the mothers of the slaugh-tered Innocents (Matt 2:16–18). Her pain was the pain of Calvary, and she was dying on the cross of her divorce. We talked, and I demanded that she pamper herself. I gave her some suggestions but rested on the bubble bath (it is my own favorite pampering).

The next day in the elevator I saw her, and she remarked that I was the priest who said she needed to party. I stopped her and told her, "No." I was the priest who told her she needed a bubble bath. Pamper not party. We smiled and went separate ways. When I returned home I went to the mall and purchased a bubble bath kit. With the help of my mom we sent the package off to one of the northern mid-western states. The package contained bubble bath (a nice lavender), some powder, and candles. I never heard a word.

One year later at the same conference the same lady came up to me on the walk. "Fr. Hector," she said. "Well, look at you," I replied. She was a different woman. She had died at Golgotha Divorce Lane, and the Lord, who loved her to the end, had resurrected her. We embraced, and she told me how she had left the conference, went back to her parish, and started a divorce re-building group. She stated that she wanted to do what I do: let people know life is greater than divorce. I asked about the bubble bath. She could not believe I had been that serious enough to send it. Her problems were still a mess, but she was not. She even brought people to the conference to experience the healing as well. She made me cry.

Time outs heal us. They allow us to see how broken we truly are. They let us look at the Divine Image again, and let it smile at us. Time outs, pausing to take inventory of who I am and how I define myself, al-low us to heal from the immense amount of damage which has been done to us by another human being and to acknowledge truthfully how we have damaged ourselves. As God knit us in the womb of our mothers (Ps 139), time outs knit us back together from all of the places we have been strewn (from lies and hurts, from abuse and rejection). Time outs give us the chance to see once again we are graced human beings who err at times but have the resolve to move our worlds to a better and healthier place. Calendaring and pampering are excellent means to move a divorced per-son from pain to healing.

CASE STUDY

The couple had been together for 6540 days given one or two leap years. The marriage had been a little shaky since the beginning. Actually the groom proposed one month after a conflict of infidelity had arisen in the courtship. Although the couple thought they had given their best over the years, divorce was obvious because too many unresolved issues in the marriage took their toll. They did love each other at some point, but little was done to maintain an intensity which would keep them together until death parted them.

The divorce put great strain on the man. He grieved his heart out at what he had lost. His depression found its outlets in all his vices: heavy drinking, heavy pornography, and occasions of promiscuity even he could not believe. His behavior was severely self-destructive. He did not love himself. Everyone was to blame for this divorce, and no one found refuge in trying to get him to focus on life again. He hoped beyond all hope that he and his "ex" would reunite. He never stopped believing he was still married even though she found a second husband. The first husband firmly believed that one day, by all that is sacred, they would find their way back to each other.

When the reality of that fanciful reunion never occurred, the man grieved still more deeply. His administrative work never suffered. His outlet for his grief was work itself. At night, however, with wine in hand he and his demons would terrorize his soul mocking him in his loneliness and drowning him in alcoholic tears. He became a master at his own pity party. He was the only guest and always the honoree. Every party ended the same: in a drunken stupor dulling his loneliness for the time being but only to wake to the absence of love.

He heard of his "ex" remarrying. He heard and made it a point to listen to any gossip he could find. Her life, her new life, still defined his. He heard of the new beau's possessiveness, of his having to dominate every move of the new couple. He heard of the wealth of the new beau and asked himself if he had been dumped because he did not have the wealth and sophistication of the new spouse. He heard joy when his "ex" related to a mutual friend that the new couple flew to South America. All he could imagine was what he was never able to offer. He relived the stupidities of his married life. He had gone to the lawyer and made a will leaving all to his ex-spouse and for no good reason. He did not have the means, nor would he ever. He listened to music and drank himself to sleep as lyrics recalled the love affair gone awry because she traded him for money. How did these songs know his life? How did they know his wife?

Friends tried to help. They told him she was never any good for him anyway. Why then did they pretend to like her in the married years? They told him to get on with life, but never told him how to erase the hurt and hope in his heart. They had many answers, but no one could see the hundreds of questions hidden in the recesses of his heart. No one had a balm for his brokenness. No one had the salve for his heart. Like Humpty Dumpty, no one could put this marriage or this man back together again.

Wounded to the core, the creative side of his spirit began the healing process within him. He would sit with his guitar, beer in hand or wine at the table, to compose music. He found himself in prayer, a strange lonely place he had known for a long time. The divorce had even ruptured his relationship with the Lord. The music, however, had a therapeutic effect on him. He found it easier to speak with God through music. His songs became prayers for healing. He never would have thought that God would have answered his musical prayers. Writing music and lyrics helped him bare his soul to God in a different way, and God found a means to reveal himself to him through inspiration. So subtle the work of God; so mysterious his means to love beyond all love. The man never realized he was being healed. He knew his music was beautiful before the Lord. He convinced his pastor and choir to play some of his music during Sunday liturgies. The music was accepted, and the man found peace when he heard his prayers sung. He also began to sense the hurt and pain in the music as well. Some songs sounded suicidal in their pleading. He realized his music was his soul. His soul was crying and at the same time singing to be healed. God was listening.

He wrote music primarily for God. He would say that his music was his prayer and that he found great solace in composing. He even had the audacity to submit his music for publication. By the grace of God, his music was published. He knew the source of the music. He knew it was from his brokenness that inspiration flowed. He knew God was listening. He knew he was being healed. He wrestled with life without his "ex". He came to understand there would be no re-union. He entered into another relationship and began to realize he had to begin a new life.

He entered counseling to address his alcoholism and his divorce. He looked at the vices which governed his life. He made hard but healthier choices. Through a great many sessions of counseling, various retreats for the divorced, the man came to define himself by terms suggested by the Lord. He stopped ceding his life over for definition from a phantom ex-spouse. In his music he found peace, and joy began to return. He even toyed with rock and roll and country western songs. It did not matter. He knew he was healing.

Then out of the chaos of life came an email across his screen. It was from his "ex". It read: "Hey I'm going to be in town." He opened up the email to read the whole message.

Hey I'm going to be in town this weekend

Would you like to try and get together for supper?

The man's heart sank. It was simultaneously the most wonderful and saddest invitation. He knew healing had occurred because he did not rush to answer. He mulled over the issue throughout the day and by chance picked up messages on another phone line he owned. There had also been a message since Tuesday from the "ex" trying to arrange the same dinner date. His heart sank further.

This was the "ex" who wanted nothing to do with him. This was the "ex" who wanted no contact whatsoever. This was the "ex" who wanted no friendship either. This was the "ex" he still loved. He knew now, however, that he could not be trapped by this game. He understood that the "ex" had never taken any responsibility for the break-up or for any of the problems in the marriage. But he so desired to see her again. And why was she making such an earnest attempt at seeing him and being together?

The man was much stronger now. His mental health had been strengthened. He had learned to define himself and not let others define him. He had learned to forgive himself for his marriage and divorce. He had learned how to pray again. With the help of his counselor, he had learned not to be threatened by relational issues. He was working on a problem in his new relationship when everything clicked to show that the problem was really about his first marriage. He could not be blackmailed. His life was worth much more than any relationship. In that breakthrough understanding, he found forgiveness for his ex-spouse and put on notice his new relationship that blackmail is never an option because it is not love. He was so ecstatic at this find he had sent an Easter card to his "ex" with no expectation of a response. He sent an invitation to a party given by his corporation in his honor to his "ex" as well again with no expected response. He knew, however, that both items were sent without having to have a response. He was healed he thought.

He had come to peace with a serious issue in their married life. A serious trauma had occurred when they were married, public enough to involve the police. Later as the divorce was occurring she accused him of never moving beyond the trauma as she had. He never argued the point, but only after he found forgiveness for her did he realize the opposite was true. He remained in his position facing the same people everyday for the next fifteen years while she changed jobs, involving much more travel while never having to face the same guilty stares of people whom she knew. It was she who had run away from the trauma. It was her pattern. When things get tough, run away. Wasn't that the marriage? Wasn't that her previous relationships before their marriage as well?

The dinner date arrived. As they were driving to the restaurant the current husband called. The man made enough of a sound so that the ex-wife would at least know he was bothered by the interruption. Were they that insecure? After all, she asked for the dinner date; he didn't.

As the dinner began, the man said in honesty, "So what are you doing here? What is all this about?"

Nothing! I just wanted to return this music you gave me to look at. It has been two years, and I realized I never acknowledged it.

I hope you are not up here trying to sell your job to me. Every time they call I turn them down probably because I am still mad at you.

I am not here about the job. I just wanted to return this music.

Did you like it?

Yes though some of it is a little . . .

Out there?

I was going to say caustic. It is about us, isn't it?

Yes! Miguel said he had spoken to you and you had mentioned that I was writing music and that you thought it was about us. I told him that if you had to think it was about us then it goes to show how shallow you are . . . If you can't read between the notes and find us . . . but then that is who you were in the relationship anyway.

No, I did not say that. I knew it was about us but in other songs you compose could you remember that maybe we had some joy too? Were there no good times? Or better yet, if any of these country and western songs make it to the top, then I get royalties.

Yes, you are the inspiration.

They laughed. Driving back from the restaurant the man stated that he had gone through some counseling. The wife had too. They talked casually until the wife began to speak about the breakup. The man turned to her and told her, "Well, you are the one who wanted out not me. This was your idea." The wife looked startled. In a blur of tongues no one could hear the other as the man reiterated his claim. The wife mentioned she could not put up with his passive aggressiveness any longer. She had gone to some psychologist where she had to confront people with whom she was angry by speaking to them in the form of an empty chair. The man thought to himself, this is the same pattern: never having to address real people or real emotions, or real confrontations. It is easy to talk to an empty chair because you do not have to listen to what it might say. It is easy to speak to an empty chair because then you do not have to recognize or acknowledge any culpability. It is easy to speak and shout to an empty chair because it is as false as the devil's tongue. It's easy to masturbate because it is all about you. Each one knew not to go further with questions or statements.

As they got back to the man's house, they went in for a glass of wine. They reminisced but the wine got to the man, and he opened his feelings.

I miss you. You know I still love you and always will. You are still my wife. I never meant to hurt you. I am very lonely without you. You hurt me when you said you did not even want to be my friend. Pray God finds me someone.

Not a word from the spouse. Silence as she watched her "ex" cry before her. The man knew this would be her response. It had always been her response. When had she truly cared how he felt? Never! But he was healed enough to be himself without her in front of her. The night ended with an invitation for him to come and visit her and her new husband. Maybe Miguel could come along and the four would make a dinner date. The man told her that would not happen. With a kiss on the cheek, the night ended, and the man reminded himself she came only to assuage her guilt.

A few days later the man sat in simple contemplation of all the events which had transpired in this visit. He could hear now the passive aggressive comment about his passive aggressiveness. He relived the startled look on his "ex" as he told her and reminded her of what she had obviously denied: that she had initiated the divorce not he. He remembered his strength in the conversation as well not backing down from the truth no matter how difficult it would be to face that truth. He had said loudly enough that he had never wanted out of this marriage. He simply did it because it was what she had wanted. He could not forget her ruse at counseling, talking to an empty chair to confront her dead father and her absent (dead marriage) husband. It angered him as he faced the cowardly way of justification she had used instead of talking with him. What was she afraid to hear? Perhaps by hearing her own voice she could continue the lie of justification for what occurred at her initiative. The marriage may have needed ending, but he was never given the chance to explore other possibilities. If things had been so rotten, why then had she come back for a Saturday night chit-chat?

With all his attempts not to judge her motives, he could only come to the conclusion of assuagement. Her guilt hit on some level, maybe through a song lyric because he was sure she had not played them all (too painful). Her actions betrayed her. She who wanted nothing more of the relationship now envisioned an everything is all right get together (*i.e.,* I am free of all guilt without ever acknowledging my culpability). Her pattern was the same now as in the marriage. Now in the divorce she still could not see, much less acknowledge, she had damaged him, too. It was easier to tell an empty chair how she had been damaged.

PASTORAL RESPONSE

One of the most difficult Sundays to preach is the Feast of the Holy Trinity. Priests coming off Eastertide are confronted with the ever-present base of our Christianity. The Trinity, however, presents homiletical difficulties because preachers often fail to begin at the beginning. Having told the story of the passion, death, and resurrection for weeks (though it is the same story for fifty-two weeks), preachers many times come up with empty hands when they are faced with God in three Persons, Blessed Trinity. I recall one of my associates remarking about his homily for Easter Monday. The parish had celebrated the Holy Week with such intensity and numbers of people we knew who had been crucified. It was resurrection we were searching for ourselves. Because he had the daily morning Mass on Easter Monday, he decided to tell the faithful: "if you do not get it by now, then go home!" Young and handsome enough, he could pull it off.

The Trinity, however, poses different questions and becomes a field of mines and potholes as one attempts to explain or justify the dogma. St. Patrick used a three-leaf clover. Preachers have used different types of gimmicks like interchangeable rings of three or oceans into pails of water to get the point across, but nonetheless, the Trinitarian doctrine is relegated to the full sense of mystery: that which we can never fully understand and that which we can never know enough about.

The beauty of the Trinity is not that we were meant to understand it. The beauty is that we have been called to live within it. This point, so simple yet so complex, is at the heart of the definition of who we are as adopted sons and daughters of the Living God. We define ourselves by that Trinitarian formula every time we begin and end our prayer with the sign of the cross. It is the ever-present statement to the world that we believe in God who is Father, Son and Holy Spirit—one in three persons. It is always edifying to see the professional athlete bless himself before he swings his bat, his arm, enters or completes his performance in whatever the sport may be. Whether he understands its entire significance is immaterial because it is a simple acknowledgment of a higher power who by faith has a relationship with the athlete and vice versa.

This is engagement and definition. This is Trinity, engagement and definition. The letters of St. John are emphatic about God being love. St. Paul in his first letter to the Corinthians chides them and reminds them of the importance of love in the Christian community (1 Cor 13). He details all the attributes of what love is and is not. It is not too far-reaching to substitute God for each love that is mentioned. If God is love (1 John 4:16), then God is patient and kind. God is not jealous. God is not rude or self-serving. God does not rejoice in the shortfalls of others. God seeks the good of the other. God believes, trusts, and hopes in us because God is love and loves us.

It is in this understanding that God engages us that we might share his life. We have been called to live in the richness of the shared love of Father, Son, and Holy Spirit. We have been filled with every spiritual blessing, and yet we still seek other solutions. God has taken us into the mystery of his life and given us a life in abundance: a life far beyond our physical one. We have been loved once and always.

The letters of St. John remind us that our starting point as a Christian person is not that we love God. Our starting point is that God has loved us first (1 John 4:10). When we reflect on the mystery of God in our life, it is this point which teaches us that God has engaged us in a life conversation with himself. Our lives have been brought into the dialogue of love among the three divine persons. The mere fact that God has loved us first is the tell-tale sign that our life is a response to being loved by God. It takes us years to realize this. My life, my words, my actions are the response I give back to God after he has told me that he loves me.

This very humbling point of self-awareness should convert our hearts to sinless virtue. Having been loved by God to the point of death, even death on a cross (Phil 2:5–11), should awaken within us the desire not to lie, not to cheat, not to steal. We should have no other God before us, to see Christ in the poor and marginalized, to work for justice, to respect life outside of the womb as well as within. God has engaged us. By faith he has whispered in our ears that he is in love with us. Patiently he waits for our lives to whisper back our love for him. When lovers love, however, it is not a whisper. They shout it with all their actions so that everyone is aware of their love. God has begun the shouting, and waits to see if our lives shout in return that we are in love with him.

Engagement draws us into the divine life. Engagement is to be in on the constant conversation of God the Father, Son, and Holy Spirit. When we listen, we cannot help but be healed. When we hear their voice, we cannot help but be forgiven. When we are forgiven then we can forgive.

The man in the case study became engaged in conversation with God. Through prayer and faith he came to realize the love God had for him from the beginning. Realizing he had been drawn into a deeper mystery than marriage or divorce, he slowly and painstakingly came to respond to God. Through his music he could hear his own plea and know that God was his healer. Through music, he came to see the Way, who is truth and life so that he might confront the lies he told himself and the lies told to him. Through music that touched the feelings of his soul, he became emotionally stronger realizing his first love had started over 2000 years ago on a cross. His decision to address that love and its consequences gave him the fortitude to face the truth about his broken earthly relationship. It gave him the courage to speak the truth to himself, his "ex", and not an empty chair. His music gave him (and still does) the spiritual strength to embrace all of life through the lens of the Trinity. God, through music, engaged his adopted son (and still engages him) to take his place at the table and join in on the eternal conversation.

The Trinity is also definition. The simple sign of the cross not only reminds us that God has engaged us in a dialogue of love, but it also serves to define us as who we are in this world. Because we too often take it for granted and sloppily bless ourselves with a rapidity as quick as a scurrying mouse, we fail to see that this gesture engulfs my entire being. I live in that sign of the Trinity. The Trinity, by no merit of mine, has made a conscious decision to include me in its relationship. I, therefore, am defined as belonging to the Paschal Mystery.

I have died and risen. I have one foot in the kingdom of heaven and my other foot is in the kingdom of heaven on earth. I have been filled with every spiritual blessing in the heavens for the grace of God has been poured out on me (Eph 1:3–4). One of the most beautiful rituals of our Catholic faith occurs at the rite of welcoming the inquirers into the catechumenate. It is the signing of the catechumens. A sponsor signs each catechumen. They are given, literally given, the sign of the cross for every part of their body. It is a marvel to see how each person is reminded that their life is now hidden in Christ and that Christ's life will be manifested through them (Col 3:3).

The Trinity defines who we are in this world. St. John cautioned his little flock not to worry what we shall become when we pass from this life to the next. On the contrary, we were taught to rejoice in what we are now: children of God (1 John 3:1–2). If the world does not know us then so be it, for it never knew our Savior, our best Lover. We, however, have felt him stir in our hearts and change our lives (Luke 24:32). We have seen his greatness and felt his forgiveness. We have touched the divine, seen the face of God, and have lived. Imagine how our lives would rejoice in healing if we lived from the paradigm of being the son or daughter of God. God has no shame in claiming us; for this he sent his Son. The difficulty lies in our claiming God.